WORLDS
APART

WORLDS
APART

AN ALTERNATIVE JOURNEY
TO BECOMING A MODERN MAN

RONAN BRADY

MERCIER PRESS

MERCIER PRESS
Cork
www.mercierpress.ie

© Ronan Brady, 2020

ISBN: 978 1 78117 682 5

A CIP record for this title is available from the British Library.

Printed and bound in the EU.

To Michelle, my family,
and all those whom I've met along the way.

Keep going and keep growing.

CONTENTS

PREFACE

In the interests of strict honesty, I can honestly say
that all of what follows is strictly honest.

However, in the interests of strict accuracy, it's important to
state that not all of what follows may be strictly accurate.

I've written it exactly how I remember it.
What my memory has done to it in the meantime is
anyone's guess.

Best of luck.

ONE

SHOULD I STAY OR SHOULD I GO?

(The Hamlet dilemma or Gwyneth Paltrow in *Sliding Doors* and the unintended consequences of cause and effect.)

I'm not going, I said.

Aren't you? he said.

No. I'm fucked.

That's fair enough then. Don't go.

I won't.

Good.

I was having this conversation with a mate and colleague of mine in the mezzanine lobby of a theatre in Letterkenny. It was a June morning in the summer of 2016 and below us the theatre café bubbled pleasantly with the chatter of locals who, for the most part, were completely unaware that at this very moment, in this very building, people were learning to fly.

By learning to fly, I don't mean planes or helicopters or any kind of typical aviation. I mean aerial circus. Aerial circus is anything that happens in the air using traditional circus apparatus like trapezes and ropes and the like. When you think aerial circus, imagine something as impressive and inspiring as Cirque du Soleil but, in the case of people like me, done on a much smaller scale.

This was why I'd made the trip to Letterkenny. I had been learning to fly for a few years now, and the two-week training festival that takes place here every year is the best place to do that in Ireland.

But right then, I wasn't thinking about flying. I was thinking about exhaustion.

We were discussing whether or not I should drive back to Dublin to take part in a photoshoot for a new circus show in which I'd been asked to perform.

I didn't want to go, I was too tired, and my mate was agreeing with me.

Fuck 'em, I said.

I mean, he continued as he paid most of his attention to his laptop, they're just acting the bollocks, aren't they?

They *are* acting the bollocks.

Cheek of them, like. Not even paying your petrol!

I know. *And* I'm knackered.

You are. You need to look after yourself, Ronan. You'll end up doing yourself an injury.

I needed to look after myself because I was a circus performer – sort of.

I say 'sort of' because I was still very unsure of myself at that time. For a while, since I first began to noodle around with circus back in 2012, I'd been nagged by the idea that I would like to *become* a circus performer. For real. Not just for fun or as a hobby, but as a profession, as a living. This idea had led me to a place where I'd taken a year-long career break from my position teaching engineering and metalwork in Swinford Secondary School. A year out to go and explore this performing thing.

I was only at the start of the career break, but already it was beginning to dawn on me that I didn't think I even *wanted* to go back teaching. Not just yet, anyway. To hell with my bank balance and the prospects of a steady career. Here, with this circus stuff, things were just starting to get interesting.

The festival I was attending is the best opportunity to train and learn new skills for circus each year. But it's tough. It demands everything you've got physically, mentally and creatively. I was almost at the end of the first week of its two-week run, and it had been a long week; a long month, really, in a long year that we were only halfway through. Already my body was beaten and I felt exhausted.

Added to which was the fact that I'd been forced to make the trip by car from Dublin to Donegal twice already in the previous three days – four hours each way. I'd done this because when the opportunity for temporary employment and the training festival collide, as Murphy's Law dictates that they must, this puts performers like me in the unfortunate position of having to attempt to do both things at once. This is the circus world, after all. We're supposed to be good at juggling, aren't we? I could worry about sleeping at some other time, in some other life, maybe. For now, I had to work from each end of the candle, take the opportunities for work and try to fit the festival around them.

I'd managed it. Twice. Just about. I was shattered, but I'd managed it. Then the possibility of this photoshoot cropped up and made things complicated … *more* complicated.

Under normal circumstances I wouldn't have hesitated to accept. But these weren't normal circumstances. All I wanted to do was train and sleep. Which is why I was seriously considering saying no.

No, however, is a problem for people like me. There is a fear of saying no that haunts all performers, just as it does all the self-employed people of the world. Self-employment is an unreliable mistress and saying no is dangerous. If you say no to the wrong thing at the wrong time, then, who knows, you might be unwittingly saying no to the biggest break of your career, something that might help pay the mortgage or, as was the case for me, give me the opportunity to even *begin* dreaming of something as fanciful as a mortgage.

This photoshoot, though, I said in an attempt to talk myself around. It might be a bit of craic.

It might, my mate allowed as he continued to work at his laptop. But …

He left the word 'but' to hang in the air between us like a bad smell. He didn't need to say what came next because we both already knew.

You see, in practice, my previous two trips to Dublin that week had required getting up extremely early and, first, attempting to unknot the mess of my body so that I might be able to face the day ahead. It's always like this. I need to get myself moving to flex the joints, to chip the rust off the hinges, to work out the kinks in the muscles that have begun to settle and ferment since the previous day's abuse.

I've always been a physical guy: strong when it comes to sports, stubborn and forceful when it comes to circus. I come in at just under six feet in my socks, and I weigh somewhere around fourteen stone. A solid slab of the rarest Roscommon meat is what I am and, as such, my natural tendency is to throw myself – some would say recklessly, others would say enthusiastically – into whatever I've set myself to.

By doing this over the course of my life so far, I've managed to ding myself up quite a bit. It means that I often wake up in that middle ground between being sore and being in actual pain. I need to get up early and start moving in the hope that, once the juices begin to flow, I'll be able to ignore my moaning body.

Following that, and after a quick dose of caffeine and food, I'd make my way to the festival to do as much of the training that day as I could before the time to head to Dublin arrived.

Circus is a wonderful world of ropes, fabrics, trapezes, hoops, harnesses and wheels, all of which are custom-designed to inflict as much discomfort as possible on anyone stupid enough to attempt them.

Don't misunderstand me, they're fantastic. They allow for a freedom of movement and a joy of expression that's not easy to find elsewhere, but they're also cruel and unrelenting. You're grinding skin and muscle off wrought steel and iron, aiming for speed and grace, but usually ending up with failure and a fall. There's not a single circus performer out there who doesn't have a dubious relationship with pain. It's part of the job. You cannot avoid it.

But I was eager to learn, and every piece of new apparatus was another opportunity to test myself and find out what I could do.

So I did as much as I could.

Once the day rumbled into the afternoon, I'd leave the festival and cram myself, my circus gear and some other performers into my clapped-out VW Golf. Then we'd eat road towards Dublin in time to perform.

Once there, I did my bit: a full-on, physically demanding circus act that brought me deep into the Dublin night-time. Afterwards, I'd turn right back around and make the return trip to Donegal. In the wee hours of the morning, I'd drive with my fellow performers collapsed unconscious in the car around me, arriving back in time to do it all again the very next day.

I'd done this twice already this week, and now this photoshoot was trying to coax me back there for a third round trip. I didn't know if I could.

Right so, I said. Fuck the photoshoot. That's the decision made.

Good, he said.

I feel better now.

I'm glad.

Thanks for your help.

Not a bother. Any time.

Cool.

The photoshoot I had now decided to skip was to help publicise a show that would be part of the Dublin Fringe

Festival. The Fringe was great, and this show would be a big deal for me, though I was not entirely sure what it was about, who the people who had asked me to participate were, or how involved in it I would actually be. It was an opportunity, for sure, but it was not the be all and end all, and since they were not paying for my time or my fuel to get myself to and from the event, I was feeling pretty good about my decision to say no to it.

I got up to leave the theatre lobby, planning to go back to my accommodation and take a snooze. Even if I skipped the photoshoot, it was only morning and there was still more work and more training scheduled for today right here. I needed to rest before I tended to that. My eyes were already closing.

I meant to ask, my mate said while he tapped away at his laptop.

Yeah?

What's their name?

Who's name?

The company. For this photoshoot. What are they called?

Dunno. This is Baby. Baby Pop Pop. Something like that.

As I turned to go, I noticed that my mate had stopped typing. For the first time in this conversation there was a pause.

I half-turned back to him. A strange look passed across his face. I was pretty tired, so I could have imagined it. I'd involuntarily fallen asleep more than once already today.

Do you mean Thisispopbaby? he asked.

Oh! You've heard of them.

I was surprised. I'd never heard of them. But performing was still relatively new to me. I'd no idea who was supposed to be who within the Irish arts world. This mate of mine had worked in the arts for years. He had a better grasp of these sorts of things than I did. But still, I had just assumed the company was small and unknown. After all, they were asking *me* to perform for them, and I was a nobody. They couldn't be big. If they were big they'd be working with somebody else, *anybody* else.

There was another pause, enough to make me feel a little uncomfortable. I turned back fully to my mate.

I'm sorry, Ronan, he said.

Sorry for what?

I need you to completely disregard everything that I've just said to you.

Excuse me?

You *have* to go to that photoshoot.

No, I don't.

Yes. Yes, you do. This photoshoot could be a massive opportunity. You have to go.

I grunted like I'd been punched. This was not what I wanted to be told.

No, I said. I *don't*!

Yes, he said, you do.

My mate didn't realise it, but I was beginning to get angry with him. Defensively angry, like he was to blame. Like it was him who was personally denying me my hard-earned rest. I squared up to him, my shoulders set to menace. Thankfully, he was not paying any attention to the fire in my eyes or the crackle in my knuckles.

Look, I said, the words grating through my bared teeth. We've been through this already.

No, he said. I didn't realise that this shoot was for This-ispopbaby. You should have told me that first. That changes everything.

No, it doesn't.

Yes, it does.

Why does it?

This is a big opportunity. This shoot will go everywhere.

What do you mean everywhere?

I mean everywhere.

But I might not want it to go everywhere.

My mate shook his head at me like I was just not getting it. Which was true. I wasn't.

I'm sorry, he said. I really am. But you're going to this photoshoot. You have to. There is no other option. I'll drive you there myself if necessary.

That was a lie. He wouldn't be driving me anywhere. He was knackered too. He helped run this training festival. He was not really working on his laptop, he was just trying to look busy, so nobody came to bother him. But I looked at his face. He was not messing about the rest of it. He looked sad for me. He understood how tired I was. If he'd been looking at me in any other way I don't think I would have taken this sudden change of advice seriously. I think I would have just ignored him. But there he was, sat back from his computer, his hands folded in his lap, looking for all the world like the Virgin Mary, eyebrows creased and upturned towards me in a vision of care and understanding.

I felt that sinking sensation of things being decided for me. I was just a passenger here, along for the ride.

Fuck, I said, my shoulders slumping.

Sorry, he replied.

I'm just so tired.

I know you are. But it'll be worth it. Trust me.

I didn't trust him. Not right then. I was too tired for trust. But I'd do it anyway.

***

A few hours later I was in my car. My body was going through the motions, changing the gears as Lifford turned into Strabane, then Sion Mills, then Omagh, then Emyvale, then Monaghan and on and on. I drove from habit, my body sore and cramped in the driver's seat.

You can always tell when you cross the border between north and south. It's not the signs and the brickwork that are different, or it's not *just* the signs and the brickwork that are different; there's a distinct feeling between the two places, a palpable shift in atmosphere. One place is a little looser around the edges than the other.

I've always thought this, and noticed it dimly again as I passed from one to the other and back again. I began to wonder, as I always did, if this was a cultural thing or a historical one or maybe even both, but my mind quickly reverted to blankness, without the energy to support such higher brain function.

So I drove, steadily making the distance between myself and Dublin shorter, keeping myself alert because, as the road signage scoldingly reminded me: *Tiredness Kills*.

No shit.

The photoshoot was scheduled to happen in some old Georgian house near King's Inns in the city centre. I didn't know who else was going to be there. I didn't know what I was walking into. And I was doing my best not to think about it. I was going. That's all that really mattered. I'd deal with what I found and *who* I found once I got there.

One thing I did know is that I'd received an email request for measurements from a costume designer a week earlier. I'd never met this person before, but it was a terse communication containing a laundry list of demands: height, chest, waist, hip, leg, thigh, knee, calf, waist–knee, waist–floor, nape–waist, cross back, collar, top arm, arm length, wrist, head, hat, shoe. I had no idea that this was the sort of thing other performers had on hand, ready to go at the merest hint of a need. I'd had to ask some of the people I knew at the training festival to help me out. They'd clucked at me, making me feel all the more like the country-boy rube I was. Then, with tape measures in hands, they had helped me put my body down on paper; every last diameter, girth and length of it.

I had thought that I was pretty okay about my body: measuring it, tracking it, improving it. I used to train every day for football, which involved minding my calorie intake, monitoring my recovery, tracking my reps and my progress. But for some reason this felt different: worse, more invasive. I'd even felt mildly violated just being asked for such information.

Sullenly, I allowed myself to be measured, then sent back the list to the costume designer with a suitably terse reply, just so they would know that I too could be brusque. But I was not happy about the whole affair. Which set me to thinking: why was I so put out?

As the drive meandered its way to Dublin, I began to think about this again. There was a little pit in my stomach that was churning with tiredness and something else that I could only identify as fear.

I had to admit to myself that a lot of the negative feeling I'd been experiencing about this photoshoot, and about the arts world in general ever since I had given this career break a go, could be put down to fear: my fear about the choices I'd made, the direction I was pursuing and the people who surrounded me. It was not the first time that I'd felt like this, but it was stronger this time. And I thought I knew where it was coming from.

This performing world was a strange one and, in all truth, I didn't know what to make of it. All these new and supposedly 'arty' people. I just didn't know how I felt about some of them. I really didn't.

They were certainly different from the people I grew up with around the rural communities of home in Roscommon, or during my college course in Limerick, or in the staffroom of the school I taught at in Swinford, or in the ranks of the FCA when I was part of the army reserve.

Rationally, I could understand that, beneath it all, everyone is basically the same. We are all human. We all act in more or less the same way. We are all driven by more or less the same motives. We all feel more or less the same things in more or less the same way. All that ever changes is how we dress these things up.

But these arty people really did dress it up differently. I mean, they were not fucking around.

Sometimes it could be like staring at a different species. Which was really confusing. All the people I knew from school, home and football, they were all recognisably similar to each other, if not quite the same. But these arty people almost seemed like they'd intentionally scrubbed out every last ounce of familiarity just to make people like me, country boys from the boglands, understand how little we comprehended about them or their world. It was like they were saying, 'Well, we never belonged to your world so, by God, you're not going to belong to ours either.'

That's an entirely unfair thing to think, of course, but this didn't stop me from thinking it.

All of my steps into the circus world so far had been small and sequential. I was that nervous kid on the beach, hands clasped to his chest, skin puckered with goosebumps as he lowers his body into the sea one gentle wave at a time, letting the chill settle through his skin before lowering himself a little bit more.

First I did a class in 2012. It was a small, contained class in a warehouse on the edge of Carrick-on-Shannon, where I learned some of the basics of aerial circus. It seemed like fun. I was recovering from a football injury at the time. My body was pretty banged up from years of playing and training with Elphin for club and Roscommon for inter-county football. It had gotten bad enough that I'd decided to take a year out to let my body catch up with itself. I'd found out about the circus class and thought that it might be a bit of craic. I'd get to learn to use my body differently, while still letting my injury heal and keeping my fitness up.

Before that, my only previous contact with the circus was probably similar to that of most people in Ireland. As a child, I'd occasionally been brought along to one of the traditional touring circuses. I'd watched the clowns, circus tricksters and the animal processions from a flip-down, plastic seating bank while I stuffed my face with popcorn and candyfloss, then I'd gone home, high on sugar and awed by the spectacle, and not really thought about it again. That's no slight to traditional circuses. They do some amazing work, but I was a young kid from a rural home. The circus was a brief delight of my childhood that came in between the serious business of sports, sports and more sports.

This aerial circus thing seemed a little different, though, and I was intrigued. I'll come back to this properly later on, but, in brief, I did the class and enjoyed it. Then I did a full-length course and enjoyed that. Then I did the training festival in Letterkenny – the Irish Aerial Dance Fest, or IADF for us veterans – and found myself eager for more. This continued, one thing rumbling on to the next, until I suddenly found myself performing: a short sketch here, a small act there, nothing too scary. Nothing that might have frightened me off. Nothing serious enough for me to have said at any time that I was making a conscious decision to pursue performing – that is, until I was actually doing it, performing more and more until I was almost entirely separated from my old life. I had entered into this new one, this arts one, while only sort of acknowledging that it was happening at all.

And even with that drip feed, that cautious approach, still the world and the people who inhabited it were strange to me. They were fascinating, but strange, and they took a lot of getting used to.

Even my first IADF had been a shock. It was great, but it was a shock. Coming from my 'normal' world, it looked to me as if I had entered into this strange-smelling, strange-eating, strange-looking, hippy-dippy, touchy-feely community that clung to the edge of a town, on the edge of a county, on the edge of a continent. They seemed a fringe of a fringe of a fringe.

I mean, what the fuck was quinoa?

I didn't know. I'd never considered anything without meat to be a proper meal, and yet here were these entirely plant-based people. I just thought that they were weird. I can't say it any plainer than that.

Yet their strangeness was alluring. It was something I wanted to learn more about, to understand and, where possible, to embrace.

But there was a cost to my curiosity. A large one that I had never, *would* never, have been able to foresee before I began this journey. The cost was that I was going to have to slowly rip out my internal wiring and reinstall it. I had preconceptions and biases and learned behaviours, a whole myriad of attitudes, all of which were completely normal for me back where I came from, but which were entirely inappropriate for this new world and these new people with whom I was circulating.

As I drove towards the photoshoot for Thisispopbaby, in this strange place with these strange people, I was struggling with all of these things.

Because, and here's the crux of the matter, a good deal of my discomfort stemmed from the fact that these were people that a past version of myself would not have liked. These were people that a past version of myself would not have associated with. These were people – a lot of whom grew up being mocked, bullied and largely led to feel excluded because of their differences – that a past version of myself would very likely have ridiculed for those same exact reasons.

Would I have bullied them? Probably.

Did I bully them? Probably.

It's hard to remember, but it seems safe to assume that I did; at the very least, I definitely did not stand up for them when other people did. But I don't want to fudge it. I don't remember bullying them because most likely it simply did not seem important enough for me to commit it to memory at the time.

Of course you *would* bully them. Why wouldn't you? They

were different. They were hard to comprehend. They were just easier to put under the boot than everyone else while we all squabbled with one another within the mad social scramble that is growing up through a conventional schooling system. I was just the same as everyone else; I was largely concerned with figuring out what was generally thought of as normal so that I could become it, attain it and then maybe find the comfort, and the privilege, that accompanies it.

And now I was trying to embrace these people?

Why?

What was I doing to myself? Why would I ever give up all that I had worked so hard to achieve: my position as a teacher, my sporting ambitions as an inter-county footballer, my life in general – why would I sacrifice it for something I didn't properly understand and could only partially explain?

I didn't know. Which made me afraid. Which made me defensive.

This fission between the stasis of my old life and the change of my new one was having its best lash at me, and it was doing a pretty good job of it.

I drove on, regardless.

***

I arrived into Dublin at some point in the early evening, my car travelling against the home-time commute of all the other 'normal' people.

I eyed them in their queues and tailbacks as I drove by. I could still be one of them, I thought. It was not too late. The comfort of a good car, some drivetime radio, an evening spent doing whatever the hell I felt like, free from worrying about the solidity of work and where my next rent payment might come from – it was all deliciously alluring.

And I could go back there if I wanted. No problem. My teaching job in Swinford was waiting for me. There was no bother. I could slip back into my old life and commit myself to the position I'd worked so hard to attain. I was reasonably good at it, and I did enjoy it, mostly.

Some things were certain with it. Thanks to the glories of the Irish payroll system, I wouldn't have to worry about assessing and paying my own taxes. That was a major boon compared to life as an artist. I would also know exactly how much I was going to earn in any given week, which was currently impossible. Things like mortgages and pensions would all be real and achievable things for me, which was not going to be the case in my new profession.

Banks look at performers the way doctors look at genital warts; they are something to be quietly removed and then never discussed again. Did I really want to spend the rest of my life as the social equivalent of a crotch infection? Surely not.

Just turn around and go home, I thought. You can finish the career break, knock a bit of craic out of it, then go home and do things properly.

Michelle was at home, back in Athlone. She is the woman I love. I could just go home to her and put this all behind me. After all, she had been somewhat putting her life on hold for me. We had been talking about homes and families and the future before this circus lifestyle that I had suddenly chosen came along. It wasn't exactly part of the deal. Not that there *was* a deal between us, but when we'd first met she had been training as a scientist and playing as an inter-county footballer with Leitrim, which isn't a million miles away from what I was doing. We never actually stated to each other that we wanted to be a conventional couple with traditional jobs and hobbies, but for a long time it did look like that was going to be the case. This new life of mine, however, meant that I would often be poor and have to be away from home for long periods of time. Rarely has work cropped up where I could be based in Athlone, which is not exactly the cultural capital of Ireland, I am sad to say.

She was there now, living her life, probably not entirely sure where exactly in the land I was. I mean, sure, she knew about the training festival, obviously. And she knew that I'd been complaining about this photoshoot, but she didn't know that I'd decided to go, that I was tired and on the road and missing her. Increasingly, this was our life together. And it was hard. For both of us, in different ways.

I drove on, fuelled by stubbornness rather than conviction, and arrived at the photoshoot tired, sullen and thoroughly pessimistic. After abandoning my car in an overpriced multi-storey, cursing the fact that here was another fifteen euro I would never see again, I found my way onto a street of terraced Georgian houses that stood proud, three-storeys tall and lording it over the plebs on the pavement. The door to one was open, with plenty of suitably strange-looking people flowing in and out. There were glitter and wigs aplenty. This had to be the right place.

I approached and attempted to introduce myself to someone climbing briskly up the steps with an armful of bric-a-brac, hurling helmets and sequinned underpants that I presumed – that I *hoped* – were for set-dressing.

Excuse me, I tried, but they ignored me and walked into the house.

I looked around. Everyone else had disappeared inside. I had no choice but to follow.

The house was a grand old darling: wooden floors with rugs running along the corridors and up the stairs.

A harried-looking man dressed in black, but wearing a pair of sparkling emerald runners that Dorothy from *The Wizard of Oz* would have been proud of, came barrelling around a corner. I decided to try again.

Excuse me, I said.

He stopped and looked me up and down, seeming mildly disdainful of what he saw.

Yes? he replied impatiently.

I'm here for the photoshoot.

Who are you?

Ronan. I'm the circus guy.

Ugh, he scoffed, turning away. Second floor.

Well fuck you! I thought. Fuck. You.

Thanks, I said, shouting after him as he disappeared into the depths of the building.

I trudged upstairs, my circus gear slung over my shoulder.

Then I walked into what I could only describe as barely contained pandemonium. There were make-up artists, drag queens, half-naked performers, tracksuit jackets, statues and old portraits of stern-looking white men, sequins, food tables, shouting, people running to and fro, and, crawling all over it all, photographers, three of them twisting themselves into various interesting positions in order to set up shots and work out angles.

I stood for a moment in the doorway and tried to take it all in. I was used to a certain degree of chaos. You could not teach teenagers or be part of a football team without being open to it as a general concept. But I was so tired, and this was all quite a lot.

Suddenly, the guy in the emerald runners from downstairs appeared again.

Ronan? he barked.

I spun around in a daze.

Yes?

I'm James, the costume designer.

So this was the guy of the terse email, who, from my point of view at least, had tried to make me feel bad about my body. At least something was beginning to make sense.

Did you get my measurements? I asked.

Whatever, he said, dismissively.

Fuck you twice, I thought. Fuck. You.

Cool, I said, coolly.

He stuck out his hand, at first, I thought, to offer it in

greeting, so I raised mine in response, until I saw that he had produced the smallest, tightest set of pink underwear that I had ever seen.

Put these on, he said, turning on his heel and disappearing once again.

I held the pink pants between my thumb and forefinger as if they were soiled.

What the fuck are these? I mean, what the actual fuck are they? Is this a joke? Is it just a prank for the country boy who wouldn't know any better? Do they really expect me to put these on and parade around in front of this room full of people I don't know, people I am rapidly beginning to intensely dislike? What were all those goddamn measurements for anyway? What on earth did they have to do with anything if all he was going to do was try and pack me into a pair of underpants sized for a flamboyantly confident ten-year-old boy?

Just then some dude wearing assless chaps and a hurling helmet walked by me.

Hey, he said.

Fuck you, I thought.

How you doing? I responded from reflex.

He strode off and I watched him go, buttocks flexing as he moved.

Fuck this, I said to myself. I'm not doing this. No way.

I turned to leave.

TWO

A COUNTRY LAD

(Or jelly raids, horse handling and dubious child
safety in rural Ireland.)

I had great craic growing up where I came from. And where I
came from was Mantua in the county of Roscommon.

There are two Mantuas in the world. One is in Italy, a place
I assume to be exotically warm and beautiful. The other, my
home, is definitely not warm or any more picturesque than
your average bogland, but it is beautiful all the same. And I
had a lovely childhood there.

I mean that. It was a good time. I am who I am because of
where I grew up.

It was brilliant. I loved it. But not everyone thinks that way
about country life.

Being Irish you already have that underdog mentality
deep-wired into you a little bit. Call it a hangover from our
colonial past, but, as a nation, we tend to look askance at other
countries and moodily complain about the things they have
that we don't.

The Celtic Tiger, with all its gaudy excess, did its level best
to fatten us up and coddle us out, but even that couldn't kill
an attitude that has been hard-baked into us for centuries:
that we are downtrodden and that this is someone else's fault.

When it wasn't a tar-stripping recession, it was the Brits. When it wasn't the Brits, it was the Normans. When it wasn't the Normans, I'm sure it was the fierce Atlantic weather or the Druidic spirits of the forests or something, anything that we could view as an oppressor.

And that feeling goes deep, because it's not enough for us to play at being the underdog in a national sense. We have codified it into our social strata as well, meaning that coming from the country you look towards the towns and cities with a begrudging, bitter and barracking sense of under-privilege and suffering.

And deeper still, we do it within our rural communities too. You can be sure that the tribes from Westmeath look across the Shannon with disgust at us devolved masses rolling around amidst the turf in the bogs of Roscommon. One of our county nicknames is 'The Sheepstealers'. The Sheepstealers, for Christ's sake! Doesn't that say it all?

Fuck those guys, we say. Look at all the shit they have that we don't. Fuck them. We'll steal their sheep. That'll show them.

Not a great image to be carrying about for yourself, but you work with what you've got.

Which then, of course, goes in the opposite direction as well.

Culchie. Bogger. Hick. Bumpkin. Even redneck on occasion. I've been called all of those things. Sometimes fairly. Most times not.

I've heard the rural life being called boring. I've heard it called simple and backwards and basic. I've had people slow their speech down when they find out that I'm from Roscommon, like I might not be able to quite catch the speed of what they're saying. I've had people begin to speak louder at me, like I might be a bit hard of hearing. I don't know. It must be the chunks of peat turf that I have wedged into my ears that cause it.

Whatever it is, it's part of our national character. Which is a shame.

Growing up in the country is great craic. It is. I'm not talking about some Enid Blyton, lashings of lemonade and raspberry jam kind of rural idyll. Not at all. There's plenty wrong and there's plenty right with rural Ireland. There are aspects of my character that I've chosen to keep along the way, others that I've had to learn to leave behind, and more still that I'm still trying to figure out.

It's a work in progress, I suppose. Always will be. But it remains true that I fucking loved my upbringing. Which isn't to say that it was always pleasant. It wasn't. But the rough-and-ready nature of it all was most of the attraction.

Like this.

My Uncle Robert, who died recently, used to be always messing around with horses, going off to pony drives, acquiring animals to race, and generally filling his time with anything that had the smell of tack and horse feed emanating from it.

There was this one time that he had a horse called Cleo out in the front field of our house. We had a farm attached to our house which we worked as a family, so we were mostly surrounded by fields over which we had free reign.

Robert fancied Cleo as a bit of a goer, an animal that might be able to do some damage at the various pony drives he attended, maybe even get the better of a bookie or two, so he was training him up.

Sometimes Robert would enlist us to help him with his horse training. We'd be let onto various horses to help break them in, to give them a trot and get them used to their tack. Not a race, mind you. Nothing so dangerous as that. Just a trot. Maybe a canter, if we were lucky.

I would have only been about ten years old, but even then I was already fond of a bit of speed, so letting me up onto a horse that had any bit of spirit to it at all was like giving me the keys to a Formula 1 car and telling me to have a lash around the circuit. I was going to do damage, no matter what way you looked at it.

This particular day, Robert wanted Cleo to go out the field on a trot with the trap behind him, so he'd begin to get the feel of it. And it was this – a ten-year-old boy perched on a rickety trap, trying to pilot a horse around a field at half-tilt – that passed for top-quality training in Robert's eyes.

He'd dropped me on top of the trap and was trying to coax the horse into moving, but Cleo, the stubborn auld fecker, was having none of it. He didn't feel like going out the field today. No. He was fine and happy right where he was. Robert pulled and tugged and cajoled and pleaded, but Cleo ignored it all, choosing instead to duck his head and begin picking at some of the grass between his hooves.

Robert stood back for a second and looked the horse up

and down, his keen eyes appraising the situation. After a short while he nodded to himself and then glanced up at me.

You have a hold of them reins, do ya? he grunted.

I nodded, the leather straps firmly gripped in my sweaty palms.

Good, he said. Wha'ever you do, don't let them go, ya hear me?

I nodded again, silent and focused.

I might have been dressed in tracksuit bottoms and some knock-off football jersey, and wiser horsing folk than Robert might have been able to tell me that I was already too solid of frame for a racing life, but none of that had any importance right then. I had decided that no matter what happened next I was going to be ready for it. Cleo could buck and kick like a wild stallion, but I was not going to let go. This was it. *This* was my grand national; a chance to prove that I was in fact the 'hardy young fella' I was always being told I'd one day become.

Robert nodded and, with a meaty paw and no further word of warning, he gave Cleo's rear a mighty slap, hoping this would give the animal a bit of a scare and jump-start him into a trot around the field.

Cleo, to his credit, took off like he'd been interfered with.

He bolted and the reins snapped taut with a whip crack forceful enough to impress even Indiana Jones. If I'd had anything other than a death grip on the reins, then this whole farcical situation would have ended right there. The straps would have been swiftly yanked out of my hands and Cleo would have been free to gallivant down the field far from Robert and his high-minded notions of equine training.

But I held those reins like my life depended on it, because it sort of did.

Cleo headed straight down the field, going from naught to gallop quicker than either myself or Robert would have thought possible. He covered the length of the field in record time and I was feeling pretty good about myself. Terrified, but grimly focused and happy to be experiencing such speed.

As we neared the ditch at the bottom of the field, I tried to pull on the reins so we would slow down a bit. The trap was old. It was imperative that we slow down enough to allow the trap to make the turn. Otherwise it would be like a train jumping its tracks, we would overturn and I would be thrown out.

By that stage I'm not sure whether Cleo was even aware that he *had* a child bouncing along behind him, because he paid neither me nor my reins the blindest bit of heed. Instead he chose to continue at full speed, headlong towards the ditch, before banking sharply left just as the first strands of briar threatened to tickle his flank.

This is where things started to go really wrong.

We took the turn at too steep an angle for the trap, causing it to rear up onto its side and spill me out onto the ground, though I was still holding the reins. Robert, who had been tearing after us with all the pace that he could muster, started yelling at me from behind.

Hold on to them reins, he bellowed. Whatever you do,

hold on to them reins, for fuck's sake.

Robert's fear was that, if I were to let go, Cleo would take off on his own and we'd then have to spend the rest of the day trying to bring him back under control.

My large and furiously insistent uncle was barrelling down the field after me, yelling instructions and obscenities in equal measure. I was in no position to contradict him, so I did as I was told: I held onto the reins as Cleo dragged me along the grass behind him like a lowly extra in the final shoot-out of a western movie.

Now, unbeknownst to either Robert or myself, earlier that day my dad had put an arborist to work in this very same field. The arborist had been set the task of trimming various low-hanging branches, and felling one old and teetering tree that lived in the ditch along the far end of the field. As Cleo raced for all he was worth, and I clung desperately to his reins, we now came to this part of the field.

Cleo started ploughing through the fallen branches with abandon, crunching them beneath his thundering hooves like they were nothing more than dried autumn leaves, sending showers of bark and splinters raining down across my head and shoulders.

Hold on to them fucking reins, Robert bawled.

And so I did, blissfully unaware of what was fast approaching.

As he drew near to the tree trunk that blocked his path, Cleo didn't even bother to give me a second's warning before he gave a fine leap and cleared it with air to spare.

Think of the whale jumping the seawall at the end of *Free Willy*. Think ET sending those kids and their bikes floating over the heads of the cops and across the face of the moon. It was a thing of grace, that jump. It would have done Robert proud had it been at the point-to-point or pony drive proper. It would have caused people to clap and cheer and rush towards the bookies with their winning slips clutched tightly in their jubilant fists. Cleo would have been lauded as a fine animal, the best there was, a dutiful beast born from good breeding and the steady hand of my wise uncle Robert.

But this was not the case. By cresting that freshly felled tree trunk in our front field that day, Cleo spent his prizewinning jump too soon. Afterwards, he had nothing left to give. He would never be a champion. His day had come and gone, unseen and unheralded while he dragged a small boy through the grass behind him in a field in Roscommon.

And I, for my sins, was doomed to be just as unlucky.

I came over the trunk belly first and caught my leg on the nub of a broken branch which promptly snapped off and lodged itself deep within my shin, meaning that Cleo, to his credit, was now succeeding in hauling an overturned trap, myself and the large branch that I was impaled upon in his wake as he continued at full gallop around the field.

Hold on to them reins, Robert tried again.

Finally, I decided that Robert might not have had the right of this one. Perhaps he didn't have my best interests in mind.

It was exactly for this kind of delayed intellectual insight that I *wasn't* considered a leading academic light at school.

I let go and gave Cleo his freedom.

He galloped off across the field to pastures new, the loose reins trailing behind him. He was not to be seen again for some hours, as Robert came up behind me, panting heavily in the sunshine.

What did you let them go fer? he asked. Didn't I tell you to hold on to them?

I turned over slowly, revealing the wound in my leg. I felt that I deserved at least some concern or maybe even an apology. I'd done right by him and had paid dearly for it. I was still thinking pretty clearly at that stage, having settled into that shock period that descends for a while after an injury and before the pain comes.

Robert looked down at my leg, and inhaled.

Well, he began, you'll be better by the time you're twice married anyway.

This joke was undoubtedly intended to make me feel better, but Robert's flippant disposal of so much of my future youth, coupled with the fast-approaching pain in my leg, smashed into me at once.

I began to cry.

Robert scooped me up and I was brought back up to the house, where he quickly handed me off to Dad, saying something like, 'That feckin' Cleo, the auld fecker, he's loose now in the fields. I'll be all day getting him back', before disappearing out of the house not to be seen again within sight or shouting distance of Mammy for many a day.

I would have been crying quite hard by this stage, that

blubbering, snot-drenched sort of wail that only young children can really pull off. After all, there was a sizeable piece of wood sticking out of my shin. This seemed like a fatal situation to me. I could die.

Dad appraised me in much the same way that Robert had the horse, surveying me up and down while looking like he was trying to decide whether or not I was beyond saving. We lived on a farm. I wasn't unused to the idea of animals being put out of their misery. Maybe, at the tender age of ten, my time had finally come.

Well, he said, we'd better get you to the hospital before your mother gets back.

The hospital! Maybe there was hope. A wash of relief swept through me.

It didn't last long.

Dad put me into the family car, lying me out as flat as I could manage in the passenger seat, and then set off for the hospital.

As he pulled off he began to flip through a selection of compilation tapes we kept in the car. They were the sort of things that you got by collecting tokens from cereal boxes and sending away for them. As a group of siblings – seven of us in total, with me the second eldest – we used to play these tapes on heavy rotation, so my father was intimately familiar with them and their contents. And he had something special in mind for me right then. Something that he thought might just cheer me up.

Now, before we go any further, there is something you

probably need to understand about my dad; a vital piece of information that will help you make sense of what is to follow. And that is this: Dad was a horrendous messer in the finest of Irish traditions. He always knew how to make us laugh.

When I was young and when it came to having the craic, he was the craic-maker-in-chief. He was a big man in my eyes for creating fun situations or turning peculiar circumstances into chances for a bit of a laugh. The hint of mischief clung tightly to him. It was never far from his thoughts. So, as he flicked through the various volumes of pop songs we had amassed for the car, he knew exactly what song he was looking for.

His eyes lit up as he found what he needed, opened the cassette case one-handed and slipped it into the tape deck with the ease of long practice.

By this time, I had managed to stop wailing by clenching my teeth together tightly enough to grind them and by gripping the sides of my passenger seat until my knuckles turned white. I was vaguely aware that he was at something, but most of my energy at that point was focused on not dying.

He pressed fast-forward and waited as the tape spooled rapidly through its first couple of tracks. With unerring accuracy, he punched the play button and began to sing at the top of his lungs.

It's the fi-nal countDOWN!

The synth-laden pop classic by a band called Europe began to blast from the car speakers. My old man turned around to me, his eyes entirely off the road, one arm stretched across me, entreating me to join in.

The fi-nal COUNTDOWN!

Each syllable punctuated for full effect as he drew it up from the deepest depths of his lungs.

The FI-NAL COUNTDOWN!

Here it was. This was how he was telling me that I was going to die. Through the medium of the quintessential eighties power ballad. This was it. My final countdown had arrived, and this swerving car journey with my dad was to be my last act upon this earth.

I began to cry again.

Dad smiled, because I didn't get the joke. But he did, which was the most important thing to his mind, so he kept on singing, playing the song on repeat until we finally got to the hospital.

I didn't die that day, but I still have the scar on my shin.

And I did learn to appreciate the joke.

Eventually.

He knew I wasn't going to die. He knew that he was being very obviously hilarious. And he knew that it would be something I would look back upon and laugh.

As I grew up, I began to really appreciate this general spirit of roguery that was available to me throughout my childhood. It permeated through practically every aspect of daily life, starting with my first steps and continuing until my late teens when I finally breached the county bounds on my way to new experiences.

We looked at life in general as something to be gamed, to be hoodwinked, to be won. The bigger the risk, the bigger the reward. Because, if you weren't going to have the craic as a kid, when on earth were you going to do it?

Like the great jelly heist of my eighth year in this world.

It was the year I had been banned from drinking Coca-Cola. Why was I banned from imbibing this quintessential cornerstone of fizzy pop culture, you might ask? It was because Coke provoked in me a special kind of insanity that my parents had tolerated until they could take it no more. As my Coke dependency increased, my behaviour deteriorated into something entirely unmanageable.

You see, whenever I supped from that divine syrupy, sugary elixir, it mixed with my existing well of ferocious, prepubescent energy to form a potent concoction of pure dementedness. I would bounce off walls like a rubber ball. I would hulk out and go into orbit around our house and farm for hours at a time. During this sugar rush I was not capable of reason or forethought. I regressed into a more caveman version of myself, and nothing except time was able to bring me back down.

It became an untenable situation for my parents. So, I was banned from it. Whether at birthday parties or Communions, visits to the cousins or to Nanny Dowd's (who was Mammy's mother), I was forbidden to touch it and all the relevant parties were similarly instructed not to provide it. Coke was even removed as a line item from Nanny's weekly shopping list – an instruction which she didn't heed – and my siblings were under strict orders to not supply me with any more of it.

Which, of course, only made me want it more.

Nanny Dowd was the primary purveyor of sweet things in my childhood. She supplied us with sweets, tarts, ice-creams, pop and chocolate. Normal breakfast fare at home was cornflakes or a bowl of stir-about (porridge), but at her house you would get the fancy breakfast cereals that came in the mini variety packs: tiny boxes of Coco Pops, Frosties and Sugar Puffs that, through some strange sorcery of time and space, seemed to taste better than the bigger box versions of themselves.

And, most importantly, she kept a two-litre bottle of Coke in situ in her fridge for all occasions. For guests, you understand. It was very important.

I wanted that bottle.

No. I needed that bottle.

And I was going to get it.

Which is how myself and my cousin Gary, who was also banned from Coke that summer for reasons almost identical to mine, teamed up to steal the bottle every week.

It was a crack-job operation. A slick and fluid smash-and-grab. We got in. We got the bottle. We got out. All before anyone could see us or stop us or rat us out to our parents.

We did this for weeks, turning ourselves secretly demented on the sugar high, hiding ourselves in ditch rows and behind buildings, sipping from the bottle in the same way we would later do as teenagers with alcohol – only this was far, far superior.

And what was even better was that the bottle would be replaced every week at every new grocery shop, with Nanny just assuming that it had been consumed in the normal fashion by those who were permitted to drink it.

It was foolproof.

Until someone introduced jelly into the equation, and everything went to hell.

Jelly was the only substance that could trump Coke in my comprehensive world ranking of sugary deliciousness. Jelly even had three forms of deliciousness. You had the solid version of the stuff when it set, which was great in its own right; you had the bar of jelly before you even melted it down, but you also had the pre-solid, still-setting, liquid form of it, which was, for me, the pinnacle of the food form.

This day, I entered Nanny's kitchen as usual, with Gary keeping lookout from the doorway. I approached the fridge, wiping my palms on my trousers; I felt like a safe-cracker approaching a safe. And that is when it caught my eye. There, on top of the fridge, stood a clear bowl of green, still-liquid jelly. My heart stopped. I could get both the jelly *and* the Coke! All my Sundays hadn't just come at once: they'd come together and conjoined, Transformers-style, to create a mega-extra-very-super-Sunday extravaganza of delight.

I've never taken a speedball, that mixture of cocaine and heroin that has managed to finish off so many celebrity drug addicts, but even in my ignorance I think I am correct in saying this: jelly and Coke together was my childhood speedball. And it almost killed me.

As I stared up at the glowing, green jelly bowl, I realised that I was too small to reach the top of the fridge on my own.

I would need something on which to climb. And I needed to act fast, as our window of extraction was always small.

I began to move with the cold precision of a focused junkie. I dragged a chair over from the kitchen table and used that to gain access to the top of the fridge. I couldn't take the entire bowl away with me, I realised. That would attract too much suspicion. I would have to satisfy myself with a decent guzzle of the sweet, sweet liquid and then make out with the bottle of Coke as normal.

Gary wouldn't get any jelly, but fuck Gary. This jelly was mine.

I clambered up on the chair and stood before the bowl. I raised it in my two hands like it was a chalice and devoured as much of the contents as I could manage while still leaving enough in the bowl so as not to arouse too much suspicion.

I set the bowl down and wiped my mouth with the back of my hand. That was delicious, I said to myself. Lovely. The sweetest thing I had ever had.

Except it wasn't.

You see, I had gulped down half the contents of the bowl without even allowing enough time for the taste to register on my tongue. I'd already decided that it was going to taste amazing, and it took a while for me to realise that this wasn't the case. Not at all. In fact, it was horrible. Awful, awful stuff.

I half-gagged, teetering atop my chair, holding on to the top of the fridge for support. Either someone had made this jelly very, very badly, or this was not jelly at all.

Gary hissed at me from the doorway.

I couldn't worry about the jelly/not-jelly now. I had to re-focus, get the Coke and get out, which is what I did, carrying the weird taste away with me into the back fields of Rath-croghan.

Later that day, Grandad Dowd assembled all the Dowd and Brady children together.

Was anyone messing around at the fridge over beyond, he asked us while pointing in the general direction of my grandparents' house.

When in doubt, deny it out.

No, I said a little too quickly for comfort.

Because, my grandad continued, there's half a bowl of calf dose gone that I had left inside on top of the fridge over there.

You mean jelly, I said.

No, he replied, understanding broadening across his face. I mean calf dose.

Calf dose is a vile brew that you give to poorly calves when they have the scour. It's a nitrous mix of God-knows-what, and could have been half poison for all I knew. And I had just drunk half a bowl of it.

My better sense kicked in immediately. I couldn't keep this one to myself. Honesty now might be important, like the difference between life and death important.

I fessed up and explained myself to my grandad, who listened with his hands on his hips and a thin smile curling the corner of his lips. When I had finished, he grinned at me slyly.

I wouldn't worry about it, he soothed. You'll have a few weeks to live yet.

And with that, he ruffled my hair and set off back out to the milking parlour, the mystery of the calf dose solved.

Now, to me, a few weeks meant three. A couple of weeks was two, a few weeks was three. Meaning that I now had three weeks left to live. Period.

What it was with Brady and Dowd adults informing their young charges that their death was imminent, I don't know, but he did, and I took him at his word.

Three weeks from that day, I would be dead.

For the next three weeks, I said nothing to anyone, and instead carried around the ever-growing dread of my impending demise with what I considered to be manful silence.

I had assumed that my grandad would have informed my parents of my death date. That they would have made the appropriate arrangements and that, at the very least, I would have gotten a party or a few presents out of the fact that, in mistaking calf dose for jelly, I had unwittingly cut my life short. I obviously didn't have a full grasp of what death was or what it meant, but I thought a few party hats, some poppers and a last delicious meal of actual jelly and Coke would not have gone amiss.

But as the penultimate day before my death arrived, no one had said even one word to me about it, and I could keep it to myself no longer.

Mammy came calling me for dinner, finding me alone down by the cattle pen where we'd wash our wellies before coming into the house. I was a simpering mess of a human being curled into the back wall, gazing out over the green fields of home for what I thought would be the last time.

What's wrong? she asked.

I'm going to die, I bawled up at her in barely comprehensible language.

She was a little taken aback by this.

What are you talking about?

I'm going to die tomorrow, I insisted. And nobody cares about it.

Tomorrow?

Tomorrow!

Who told you that?

Grandad!

Grandad?

Slowly, she coaxed the story out of me until the truth became clear.

She started to laugh.

I didn't think it was that funny, but she laughed anyway. And, in fairness, what else was there to do?

Now, I fully accept that some people who read these stories may mistake them for harrowing cases of reckless child endangerment. And, to be fair, they have good cause to think that. It certainly was dangerous, and harrowing in the moment. But it is still something I look back on with a high degree of fondness, because it was that sort of boundless, high-octane, always-on-the-lookout-for-the-next-piece-of-prize-devilment mentality that coloured so much of my childhood and adolescence growing up in Roscommon.

Being able to live a life unshackled is not something that

is generally associated with rural Ireland because, of course, the shackles were hiding elsewhere and were reserved for different people in different circumstances. But I wasn't to know that then. I didn't understand the special place of privilege I occupied due to the strange alchemy of luck, birth and biology. And even now, I look back on that aspect of my upbringing, the unshackled carnage of it all, as an overall good.

Would I be saying that if I'd fallen off the trap, cracked my skull and bled out in that field with the traumatised shadow of my uncle standing above me? Or if the calf dose had really finished me off? Probably not, not least for the corporeal challenges that would present for me in writing this book, but even then, I think that I'm still grateful for having been able to get away with all the shit I pulled back then, and the shit that was pulled on me, because I don't think any of us would be able to do it now.

That might be the naive view of an older generation. Everyone thinks that their childhood was a great one and that modern life is a restrictive muddle of complications that steals innocence from the young and doesn't allow anyone to do anything anymore. But there are definitely some things that I did back then that simply wouldn't happen now.

Like the discos.

How's this for stereotypically country?

I used to drive our tractor to the teenage discos that took place every month at the local community hall in Bellanagare.

No, I'm not lying to you. I'm not making this up for

comedic effect. I'm not exaggerating for the sake of the story (although, Lord knows I do that). This is a true thing that actually happened.

Every second Friday of the month, myself and my brothers would load onto the family tractor, a Zetor 5045, dressed in the slickest and most devastatingly class outfits that we could assemble from our St Bernard's, Penny's and O'Neill's-laden wardrobes, and trundle through the back roads from our house to the Bellanagare Community Hall.

My older sister would be going to the disco as well, but she wouldn't get on the Zetor for the spin there because she didn't want to get her clothes all messed up. She would only consent to the lift home once the night was done.

The Bellanagare disco was the type of rural teenage event that was very popular in my day. I think times have probably moved on a little, taking the Bellanagare disco and its ilk with it, but I have no doubt that similar sorts of things still exist in some form and in some place, just in different forms.

The ingredients for this kind of happening are as follows.

First, acquire a big hall or venue of practically any kind so long as you can make it dark and put some strobe lighting inside. Add an overly loud sound system that can barely handle the decibel level it's going to be asked to achieve, mix in a constant rotation of the most popular and current collection of banging dance tunes (with current being far more important than good, as there's no point pulling out a classic dance hit here unless it's 'Maniac 2000' because we just don't want to know). Douse everyone with enough *Lynx Africa* and perfume to gag a gas mask, sprinkle in an unhealthy amount of surreptitiously sourced alcohol that would cause even a black-market veteran to cock an eyebrow, and finally bake for a few hours with a captive teenage audience for which this event constitutes the highest possible social gathering imaginable.

Add all of that together and what you get is an intoxicating powder keg of teenage emotion and social grandstanding. A night of activity that cannot, *must* not, be missed.

The dance hall has always been a cornerstone of the Irish mating ritual. The famous 'Ballroom of Romance' in Glenfarne, County Leitrim lay not too far north of where I grew up, and the Bellanagare disco was only the offspring of that bygone era, just with newer clothes and faster music. The essence was still the same. Pack a heap of young horny Irish folk into the one room, uninhibit their repression with the required amount of booze, and then let them run headlong at each other from across the room as if it were some form of violent competition.

This was how we, as opposite sexes, learned to interact with one another. I was lucky, I went to mixed schools in both primary and secondary, but most of the people around the area still went to places that were split by gender. For many of them, the disco was the only time you got to see a girl or a boy.

It was a vital part of our upbringing, a highlight of our calendar, a formative part of what moulded our characters, and we used to drive to it on the Zetor.

Sure, how else would we have been able to smuggle our stolen bottles of alcohol with us to the dance?

On the way there we would rattle along the back roads in the Zetor's cabin with the daylight fading around us. There wasn't a single adult who spent as much as a cursory glance upon us as we steered our hulking mass of farm machinery down the narrow, tree-canopied roads. Why would they? It was not unusual to see young people packed into every free space available on any kind of moving conveyance in order to get from A to B. That was just how things were.

We'd arrive and park ourselves out the back of the community hall where we could safely share our bottle of booze.

I was largely a good lad when it came to things like that. Alcohol, I mean. I wasn't mad after it in the way some of the others were. And I wasn't entirely stupid either. I had a vague understanding that it probably wouldn't be the best idea in the world to get myself liquored up and then let loose onto the night-time roads of Roscommon with a heap of teenagers hanging off my tractor. So, I would take a small sip of the bottle as it was passed around for the sake of show, and then let the others get down to the heavy work of adolescent inebriation. I was there for the craic and the girls and the chance of a shift, and if that meant forgoing the alcohol side of things for the time being, then that was just grand by me.

Inside the hall it was always a battleground, in more ways than one.

Not only did one have the principal concern of looking cool enough to impress whatever girl or boy you thought you stood the best chance with, but periodically a stand-off would occur between the locals hailing from the surrounding countryside and what we would have considered to be the 'townies'.

People from Roscommon town were definitely townies, there's no question. They were a hopelessly soft and ignorant bunch of city slickers. Everyone could see and agree on that. But a townie could be *anyone* not from the country as we understood the country to be. Your credentials as a true-born resident of the countryside could be disqualified for the sin of living in a place the size of Elphin, a village of less than 600 people.

In reality, you only had to live in a place that consisted of anything more than one street and fifty houses before we became inherently suspicious of both you and your mettle.

As I mentioned before, we looked at them as though they had a needless abundance of luxury. The Elphin GAA Club had changing rooms *and* showers at their local pitches. Where we were based you had to get changed at home because we didn't even have changing rooms, and it was far from showers in clubhouses that we were raised.

And that went for everything else too, begrudging every conceivable sort of facility or benefit until we got to this weird stage where we began to legitimise our lack as a benefit. We didn't need all this extra shit. In fact, we were better off without it. We were *proud* that we didn't have and didn't need these 'luxuries'. And, you know, fuck those guys.

Townies *thought* they were tough. They *thought* they were cool. They *thought* they were smarter and stronger and quicker and more sophisticated than the rest of us bog dwellers. They wouldn't take a tractor ride to the dance, wouldn't be caught dead on one, most likely. They got the bus here, with the rest of the townies. A faded white, minibus affair with more dents than a panel beater could bear and a driver teetering on the edge of alcoholism. You know, in style.

They would saunter into our disco like they owned the place, like they were doing us a favour by gracing the creaking floorboards of the Bellanagare Community Hall, like the very sheen of their haloed presence was something that we should buckle our knees for and bow down in teary-eyed gratitude.

Sometimes we would let this pass. We would shrug our shoulders and see if we couldn't get the shift from the fresh flesh that these townies provided for us. What was the summer for if not new experiences, and maybe not all the townies were that bad. After all, there were only so many people in the area you could kiss before things began to get a bit repetitive.

But there were other times where we couldn't stomach the slight of their smugness any longer. Times when we would gather in groups at the corner of the darkened hall and stock up on our simmering rage until it was just too much to stomach. At those times, there was nothing to do but fight.

Which is what we did.

Our country version of fighting was to stand toe to toe with our townie adversaries and duke it out with fists. If things got desperate, you could of course revert to using your head, elbows, knees or feet, but the first aim was to finish things with your fists if you could manage it. That was the truest form of victory. We were made of sterner stuff, after all. Sure, hadn't I almost died as a young'un with half a tree trunk sticking out of my shin? That was the sort of stock that we came from; so as far as we were concerned, fighting was hand-to-hand combat.

The townies, on the other hand, did not subscribe to this form of violent engagement. They were an altogether more sly and less honourable cohort of people, as we saw it. They wouldn't even wait to fail with their fists, choosing instead to begin a fight with a broken bottle or a shiv of a blade. We saw this as a coward's way around things, further proof that townies were softer and weaker than we were. Shivs and bottles were a luxury. And by now you should know how we felt about things like that.

As such, we took it as just added spice to the challenge to beat these fools with our hands while they tried slashing at us with their feeble weapons. We country people, we *were* weapons, dealing daily as we did with animals and weather that would as soon kill you as coddle you. Their shivs and bottles held no fear for us.

So, we'd fight each other. And it all seemed very important. At the time.

Which is another thing. I don't remember ever losing any of these fights. I certainly don't remember anybody actually getting stabbed, which at the time just seemed like further proof that these townie folk didn't know how to handle themselves but, looking back on it now, I begin to wonder how accurate my memory really is.

We couldn't have won every fight. Same too with all those knives and bottles I remember. I wonder how often they really appeared, and how often anybody actually tried using them with intent, because if it was anything like as frequent as I remember it to be, then the Bellanagare disco would have been a bloodbath, which of course it wasn't. It couldn't have been. Otherwise we would never have been allowed to go. My mother would have seen to that, if not my father or my uncle Robert. She at the very least understood the value in keeping my body intact and in good health.

But they did happen, occasionally as flashpoints on the dance floor or, more typically, out the back of the hall, away from the interruption of adults, save maybe the minibus driver if he could be roused from his stupor. Then it would be over, and we would all pile back inside to see out the night until it was time to return home on the tractor.

My sister, fresh from her latest exploits, would join us in the cabin this time for the spin home, free now from the danger of her look being smudged by the diesel and dirt of the tractor.

She has always been the wise one.

Looking back, I have a different attitude to the casual place the fighting took up in my childhood.

Back then we fought everywhere: at the dance, in school, on the pitch. Fighting was just a part of life. It wasn't something you fell out about. You'd get into a scrap, win or lose, nurse your wounds or your fallen pride, then get on with life.

Of course, that's assuming you had the ability to handle yourself, which I did. What would life have been like for me if I'd been anything other than a robust, football-playing farmer? What if I'd liked weird music (for which you can read any music that wouldn't have featured in a *Now That's What I Call Music* compilation)? What if I'd been uninterested in football? What if I'd been anything other than firmly heterosexual?

Life would have been very, very different for me.

And that's why it's hard to reconcile myself with the fact that I had a great time – because that great time was allowed by a set of circumstances that were tailor-made for me and people like me and not for people sort-of like me or people maybe like me. Because deviation was not tolerated, it was ridiculed and demeaned and thoroughly bet out of any place in which it was found to reside.

And I was okay with that at the time. I found it to be comforting even. Those rigid boundaries were like a protective barrier that kept the world simple and safe. I lived like a king. And that came at the expense of others. And just like I'm grateful for the benefits, the fact that I carry a degree of shame for some of my behaviour is just as undeniable.

Like my foray into the world of mobile-phone wholesale and entrepreneurship.

For a while there during secondary school I turned myself into a Del Boy type of character. I wheeled and dealed. I looked at the situations in which I found myself and figured ways to turn them to my financial advantage. All I lacked was the lambskin jacket, the dowdy, dim-witted sidekick and that sweet, sweet Reliant Robin as my chariot of choice.

I did have the family Zetor though, so that was something.

I grew up in that period of life when mobile phones were still finding their footing amongst the youth. The colossal grey bricks shown in eighties movies about Wall Street had been slowly replaced by the smaller, slicker models produced by luminaries like Nokia and Motorola, which eventually put them within the financial reach of secondary schoolers like myself.

Having a Nokia 3310 so you could play snake was all well and good, but as with everything during school, phones quickly became a status symbol for those seeking coolness. In order to keep up, you needed to be on top of the latest developments in mobile-phone handset chic.

In that, I was your man. Just like Morgan Freeman in *The Shawshank Redemption*, I was the guy who could get it for you.

Our secondary school only had about 100 students within it, which put me as the fourteen-year-old, black-market guru. This was galling for some of the older students, who had to abase themselves by dealing with this jumped-up little shit just to get their hands on a phone. But there was nothing they could do. I had the connection. They did not.

My connection was an internet presence called FoneFingz.

One of my mates, called Barry, was the first person to introduce me to the world of internet commerce. Using various mobile phone forums, he had already gone through the process of sourcing, buying and receiving phones from the UK to either keep or sell on amongst the local community. I was eager to learn, and Barry was happy to teach.

Barry bid me log on at a certain time so he could guide us to the requisite forum and introduce me to his primary source for all things telephonically related, Mr FoneFingz.

At the time, I had assumed that this person was a man, because my frame of reference for most things business-related was very limited, and I had thought that the term 'Fingz' stood for fingers, as in Phone Fingers. It was only some years later that it dawned on me that Fingz, when pronounced with a cockney twang, might actually mean Things.

I've told you before, I'm not always too quick on the uptake.

FoneFingz was to become our portal for getting the newest mobile phones straight from the UK, but with seriously reduced prices when compared to what would have usually been available to us in Ireland.

How we judged what was considered to be a fancy phone at the time was by looking towards our business uncles (again, men and business, do you see the pattern?), who would have bill-pay phones paid for by work. Whatever they had was typically a good indicator of what was top of the line. Movies too were helpful in trendsetting. We did a smart line in the red Nokia 8210 all thanks to the *Charlie's Angels* film of the early 2000s.

This was a time when phones were getting smaller and smaller. The smaller the phone, the slicker it was. So, through FoneFingz, myself and Barry acquired some small phones for ourselves, which quickly caught the notice of our schoolmates and neighbours.

When polyphonic speakers became a thing, we were the

first to have them. Same too with in-built cameras. We were there ahead of everyone else.

Quite soon it became a thing where other students approached us to ask where and how we had gotten these articles of extreme cool, coming as we did from less-than-cool backgrounds. Instead of delivering our secrets, we simply offered to provide a phone of their choice and budget for a modest price, still far below fair market value.

We took orders and cash payments from our fellow students in droves. Because we were too young for credit cards, and because we didn't want the oversight of our parents, we took the cash to our local bank, exchanging it for various bank drafts of differing amounts, sometimes as small as fifty euro, my largest ever order coming in just below one thousand euro. We would then amble down to the post office and, via registered post, send these weighty bank drafts off to Mr FoneFingz. Then we would wait.

The waiting was always tinged with a fair-to-middling degree of panic that this was going to be the time that we got ripped off. That this was going to be the time that our bank drafts and the hard-earned money of our customers would disappear into the ether, and we would be left to the knuckle-cracking, mob-forming mercies of our angry and out-of-pocket fellow students.

The first time I made a bulk purchase with Mr FoneFingz I was a very nervous individual, and I wanted to digitally meet this person I was trusting with my money.

Barry duly arranged for us to meet over MSN Messenger,

the preferred application for internet dialogue at the time, coming, as it did, with such things as group chats, customisable fonts and even basic smiley face emoticons – the forerunner to that staple of visual communication, the emoji.

I felt this conversation would be a good thing. I'd get to strike up a rapport with this person I was looking to make my teenage fortune with and, really, what could go wrong? I thought I was relatively with it. I thought I knew a lot about how the world worked. I thought I was au fait with the finer points of text talk as it had been developing at the time. But this all got thrown for a loop pretty quickly.

Chat begins.

Barry: Two seconds while I add FoneFingz, okay?

Ronan: Cool.

Barry has added FoneFingz to the conversation.

Barry: Hey there!

FoneFingz: Hey.

Ronan: Hello.

FoneFingz: Hi.

Barry: Ronan, this is the guy who's going to make us rich.

FoneFingz: I do what I can. LOL.

Ronan is typing…

Ronan: WTF?

FoneFingz: Sorry?

Ronan: Is this guy gay?

FoneFingz: …?

Barry: Sorry?

Ronan: LOL? Is this guy coming on to me?

FoneFingz: You know I can see that, right?

Barry: Ronan, you put that in the group chat?

Ronan: What the fuck is this LOL shit?

FoneFingz: I'm not gay.

Barry: He's joking!

Ronan: Lots of Love! How is that not gay?

Barry: Joke. See. LOL!

FoneFingz: Yeah … Lol.

Ronan: Lol is what I say to girls I'm trying to shift!

Barry: Lollollol.

FoneFingz: Shall me move on?

Barry: Lets.

We did move on. And we did make our money until the good times ended. But looking at the exchange now, it's hard to miss the mix of hyper-defensive mannishness and homophobia I was quite comfortable throwing around because, let's be clear, I was indeed very comfortable with being homophobic at the time.

It would have been unusual not to have been. Even outside of a sexual context, things that were gay were things that were defective or crappy or sentimental or fragile or emotional in some way. If you could successfully level the accusation of gayness against something, you could reduce it, diminish it.

Language is a weapon. And we wielded it as such. It took a long time before I truly understood that, and by then I was already deep into the world of performing arts, trying desperately to understand and rewire myself.

THREE

WHAT'S HAPPENING HERE?

(Paparazzi in the weeds, twenty-eight things I hate
about me and the underrated talent of ignorance.)

The inside of your own car can be a wonderful space.

It's warm, it's quiet, it's yours and it can help get you far, far away from wherever you happen to be. It doesn't ask any questions. It's not demanding. All it requires from you is some fuel and the correct key. Give it those things and it will take you anywhere you want to go.

It was to my car that I returned after James, the costume designer for Thisispopbaby, presented me with my pair of pink Y-fronts and after the assless chaps dude had greeted me so nonchalantly, as if wearing a helmet and walking with your buttocks bare was the most normal thing in all the world.

It was to my car that I *retreated*, seeking some space to collect myself and hopefully figure out what the flippedy-fuck I was doing here.

I closed the door, savouring the *thunk* sound that the door made as the rubber seals chased the last of the outside world away.

That was better.

I rubbed my hands along the rim of the steering wheel.

It was cool and soothing. It was happy to see me, and I was happy to see it.

If I wanted, I could just slip the key into the ignition, let the cylinders fire the engine into life, ease this battered piece of vehicular apparatus out of the multi-storey car park, and point myself in the direction of away. I didn't know where away might be, but it sounded like a lovely place to me.

Away.

Yes, please.

Take me to there, Mr Car.

My circus gear was thrown in the passenger seat beside me. The offending piece of pink costume wear was lying on top of the gear like a prime piece of evidence from a crime scene. From the safety of my driver's seat, I glanced down at it.

It was looking at me. I swear to God it was. As it lay there, for all purposes inanimate, it still somehow managed to come to life and *accuse* me. It said, *you might be muscle-bound and sturdy. You might think that you're tough. But, boy, you ain't got shit on me. I've seen things. And I'm not the one in my car hiding from these scary artsy folk like a little boy who's lost his mammy in a supermarket.*

I don't know how else to say this. Those Y-fronts were cruel. But they were not wrong.

Truth is like poetry, and most people fucking hate poetry.

I heard that quoted in a film called *The Big Short.* I'd laughed heartily at the time. Most people *do* fucking hate poetry, I'd said to myself, fairly confident that my relationship with the truth was robust enough, and so, in laughing at that joke, I was laughing at other people whose grasp of self-awareness was much more tenuous, other people who were there to be pitied and, where possible, avoided.

Well, these Y-fronts were saying, right back at you, Ronan. How truthful with yourself can you be?

Right then in that car, in the grey gloom of an inner-city Dublin multi-storey car park, I really, really did fucking hate poetry.

Yes! Okay, yes! I could go away. I absolutely could. There was absolutely nothing stopping me from doing that. But the question remained as to where that 'away' might be.

Would I turn around and return to Donegal and the training festival? For what? Yes, I was enjoying the training and the learning and the testing of my physical and creative limits, but if I wasn't doing it to be put into situations exactly like this one, then what was I doing it for?

If I couldn't do this photoshoot, then why exactly had I taken my career break from work? Why had I done all that if not to see where this circus life might lead me? Wasn't the idea to push myself into new and unfamiliar worlds and see what happened? To see how I'd react and what I might be capable of?

Did I really expect that all traces of the pressurised world that I'd experienced throughout my competitive sporting life before this would fall away from within the warm embrace of the performing classes? That the drudgery of my day job, a rotating collage of lesson plans, paper corrections and parent–teacher meetings would be melted into memory from the non-stop joyride that would be a circus career?

Drudgery and pressure invade everything. The trick is to understand that, to accept it, and to find something worth enduring them for.

I think there's this impression of the arts world as a cosseted, flighty place full of soft folks who couldn't or wouldn't hack the real work of daily life. It was certainly the impression that I had held coming into circus.

Look at these people, I'd think, look at them prancing around without so much as a care in the world. They're probably only feeding from the government tit in some fashion. They're either publicly funded out the rear or they're just scrounging from social welfare and only calling themselves artists, making a show of themselves for nothing else than the sheer nonsense of it. And what do they have? Not even a car to their name, I bet; barely even a bank balance to call their own. And what do they think they are doing with themselves? Nothing! Nothing useful, anyway. Nothing helpful in the societal sense of the word, that's for sure.

How this was going to be any different for me upon my flirtation with the arts world, well, I hadn't quite figured that out yet.

Either way, here I was, feeling the pressure of competition all over again. And it was in the fecking arts world of all places.

For starters, I was in competition with those people back at the photoshoot. I was being pushed into a professional scenario that I was baulking at, and yet it stuck in my craw just how *chill* with it all everyone else in there seemed to be. Why weren't they freaking out like I was? Didn't they know what they looked like? How dare they be so okay with it. Fuck them. If they could do it, then so could I! I was tough, goddamn it. I'd survived the Bellanagare disco for Christ's sake! Didn't they know what that meant? I'd fought the townies with nothing but my fists!

There was that, and then there was the competition with myself. That was even more intense.

I'd set this as a challenge for myself. Not just the photo-shoot, but this whole career break thing. I wanted to see if I could make a go of it. I had been a footballer. I had been a teacher. Turning to circus was a wild choice. The wildness of that challenge was part of what appealed to me. And while the idea of turning back up in Donegal or at home with my tail between my legs definitely did not appeal to me, the notion that I'd have to live with an eternal sense of disappointment in myself was a much more fearful prospect.

And look, don't get me wrong, this all sounds like a ludicrous over-exaggeration. I know it does. It was just a photo-shoot and a pair of pants. Suck it up and get it done. Why on earth would I be having such an existential crisis over something that, on the surface of it, seemed so small?

All I can tell you is that it didn't seem small at the time. When you're within something, sometimes you can sink so deep inside of it that the walls rise up around you and you can no longer see outside of it. Worse still, there is no outside of it. There is just you and this thing. Nothing else exists.

I was there, deep in the hole, the walls standing tall all around me. I couldn't see anything except myself and this choice. Do the photoshoot, or call bullshit on the whole thing and go home, back to your job and back to your life.

I was in competition with myself, and there's nobody on the broad face of this wide earth that I like losing to less than myself. I'm a prick to lose to. It's not pleasant. I wasn't going to subject myself to it.

So, after fondling the steering wheel longingly one last time, I got out of my car.

Back at the photoshoot, they hadn't even noticed that I'd gone anywhere. James, the costume designer, breezed past me again.

Haven't you changed yet? he asked.

No, I … I began, but James was already gone.

As far as he was concerned, I was only a very small and unknown cog in this machine, and he had other things to attend to.

I set my bag of circus gear down into a corner of the main room, away as far as possible from the chaos of set-dressers, make-up artists and photographers, and began poking around for the dressing rooms. If I was going to do this, I wanted a bit of privacy first. I wanted to get these dreadful knickers on me in the sanctity of my own presence and work up the gumption from there to step out in front of the rest of these people.

Someone who looked vaguely official happened to come striding by.

Excuse me, I tried.

They stopped.

Yes?

Where might I find the changing rooms, please?

They grinned an unwelcoming grin.

You're just going to have to find yourself a quiet corner, I'm afraid.

They pointed to the corner where I'd put my circus gear.

Over there is probably your best bet, they continued. Sorry. That's all we have.

And with that, they were gone.

I returned miserably to my 'quiet' corner, a place so private it was in view of literally anybody who might care to look and began counting to myself for want of space to think.

I've been in many a men's changing room in my life. I've seen a lot of squishy ass-cheeks and a lot of penises. I've even heard tell of the Radox challenge (a competition whereby virile young men in the crowded presence of their eager teammates get themselves erect to see how many bottles of Radox they can hang from their throbbing members) but never actually seen or competed in it because, of course, that was a thing the townies did, which only served to complete the picture of their weirdness. I'd never really had a problem before in stripping down and getting changed, but that wasn't because I was supremely comfortable in my bare skin, it was because I only ever did it in the place that was designated for changing. You were *allowed* to be naked, or semi-naked, in a changing room. The rule was that you didn't make it weird by looking or commenting on it. And I was okay with that.

However, getting changed in the corner of a room with strangers who were then going to *look* at me was a different thing altogether. I felt more like a piece of meat now than I ever had in any changing room in any GAA club anywhere in the country. These Y-fronts made me feel more exposed than if I'd been just in my bare skin.

But I wasn't going to attempt to back out again, so I returned to my corner and slowly began to disrobe.

My hope was that, if I moved as little as possible, then I wouldn't catch the attention of anyone. A lot of my knowledge of dinosaurs is based on the original *Jurassic Park* movie, like the notion that if you don't move then the T-Rex cannot see you and thereby cannot eat you. I tried to put that theory into effect now.

Practically operating in slow motion, I pulled my trousers off one leg at a time, a freeze-frame striptease with my back turned firmly to the rest of the room lest a wayward glance shatter my fragile resolve. I did the same with my boxers, hoping that no one would notice the blush invading my buttocks as they flashed themselves to the room. I slipped on the pink pants, grimacing with distaste as the material slid over my skin. I was just hoping that this thing wouldn't give me thrush, which, looking back on it now, was a less than politically correct thought to have had. Finally, I removed my top, and the change was complete.

I was now more on show than I had been warming up in Croke Park for an All-Ireland quarter final while thousands of people found their seats. I was now more on show than that time my parents had taken photos of me and my siblings in the bath and then paraded them around to any household visitor that might have cared to look. I was now more on show than at any other point in my entire life.

My back was still turned to the room, which became the next problem. The idea struck me that *Jurassic Park* might have been full of shit (fun fact: they no longer think T-Rexes' eyesight was based on motion because – and this makes sense – how could a ferocious monster that big ever have kept itself fed if that was really the case). What if, far from making me unseen, my slow-motion striptease had generated more attention?

I began to feel numerous pairs of derisive eyes boring into the deeply white Irish flesh of my back. Oh God! This was bad. I'd already made a fool of myself. And now I would literally have to turn around and face the music.

I counted to myself again, whispering numbers beneath my breath as a mantra to keep myself calm.

Consider that picture for a moment: a fully grown man dressed in ill-fitting pink Y-fronts, huddled face-forward into the corner of a well-populated room, talking to himself.

Be honest. It doesn't look great, does it? No, it doesn't. It looks like an acid flashback mash-up conjured from a wild night between *The Rocky Horror Picture Show* and *The Blair Witch Project*. I was not covering myself in glory here.

I got a hold of myself somehow – I still don't really under-stand how, because I was again close to bolting for the door, Y-fronts be damned – and turned to the room. Not one single person was looking at me. Not one.

My emotions swerved unnervingly from embarrassment

to anger. How dare they not appreciate what I'd just gone through for them. How *dare* they not understand the personal sacrifices of character that I'd just made on their behalf. This had practically been my Vietnam, and not a single soul amongst them cold manage the basic humanity to acknowledge my struggles.

I had gone full 'Don't look at me. LOOK AT ME!'

What can I say? Us humans are a contradictory bunch.

Since no one was paying me any mind, I decided to begin assembling my circus gear. My principal performing skill involves a piece of kit called a 'cyr wheel', which can also be known as a roue cyr, mono wheel, simple wheel or just a circus wheel. A cyr wheel is a giant metal hoop that was introduced as a piece of circus apparatus by a performer called Daniel Cyr in the 1990s in Canada.

If you've ever seen that famous Leonardo da Vinci sketch of the Vitruvian Man, the four-armed and four-legged dude in a circle with loads of writing around him, then that's a pretty good image to keep in mind for what someone looks like in a cyr wheel. It's an empty hoop of metal that I stand into and roll around in. I can do rolls and spins and twists and turns, the biggest and most impressive move of which is what's known as a coin-spin, whereby you spin almost flat along the ground, rattling like a coin that's been spun and is just about to land. You can either get a wheel that is one complete piece, or you can get segmented wheels that are split into sections and then fitted together to complete the hoop.

Since I was making my way in the world with nothing

but an ailing VW Golf to transport me about my business, it should come as no surprise that I could not fit a six-foot-diameter ring into the boot of my car, so I set myself to the task of constructing my segmented cyr wheel.

By the time I'd finished doing this, most of the other performing artists had arrived for the photoshoot. Aside from myself and assless chaps, there was a woman with a violin dressed in something like a harlequin dress. There was another woman with a barcode leotard and a megaphone. There was someone who looked vaguely familiar from the telly or YouTube or something whose name I couldn't place but who looked normal enough, save for a multi-coloured shell-suit jacket. And then there was Panti.

I might not have known anything about the arts world, but I knew who Panti was.

Rory O'Neill, better known as drag-queen icon and Queen of Ireland 'Panti Bliss', strode across the room in a sparkling gold-sequin dress complete with shoulder pads, voluminous blonde hair, teetering scarlet high heels and an old, calabash-style smoking pipe.

It doesn't matter where that woman is; she commands a presence. Rooms gravitate towards the centre of her rotation. And as she strode across the scuffed wooden floorboards and threadbare rugs, a hush seemed to follow in her wake.

Or that's how I remember it anyway. In retrospect, it seems more likely that I was the only quiet one there since everyone else would have known Panti for years, working with her on many, many occasions. But this is my story, and this is the painting my memory conjures up, so for the purposes of this telling, *everyone* turned to look, not just me.

By this point I had been gently ushered out of my corner-of-the-room hiding place in order to let some more photographers dump their bags and begin assembling their cameras for the shoot. This put me right in the path of Panti's stride. And in fairness, with my cyr wheel assembled and my pink pants, which strained impressively, and not unflatteringly, against the pressure of my junk, even in this artsy company I was hard to miss.

Panti half-stopped as she passed me by.

Oh hiiii, she drawled happily, giving me the old once-over.

Cleo, the old fucker, I remembered him then and I finally understood what it must have felt like to be appraised by the sharp eyes of my uncle Robert.

You'll do just fine, she continued, before turning on her heel and continuing on her way.

It would not be unreasonable to assume that I should have been extremely complimented by that exchange. Panti is very good-looking, and very well known, and she was telling me that I was also good-looking and, more importantly, that I fitted in nicely with everything that was going on around me. My Y-fronts, the wheel, everything; I was cool. Panti said so. All positives for which I am now very grateful. But that was not how I reacted at the time.

At the time it was just one more reason for me to pack my things and leave. Fuck all of this noise. I didn't need it. I didn't *want* it. I didn't *want* to be ogled by a stranger like a piece of meat and told that *I'd do just fine.* They could have it all. I was outta here.

I was going to leave. Again.

God, this was getting tedious.

The only thing that really saved me from bailing out of the whole scenario was that nagging Irish concern with not causing a scene. There was no clean exit because I'd have to try and get changed out of these pervy-pinkies unless I wanted to be done for indecent exposure out on the street. Meaning that if I tried to leave, everyone would see me doing it; they'd come and try to talk me out of it. The scene would be excruciatingly unbearable.

I wasn't able for a scene. I didn't have the energy. So, in the aftermath of Panti's 'compliment', I just shut my mouth and choose to seethe inwardly instead.

You know, the healthy Irish approach to such things.

Shortly afterwards, I was escorted over to the make-up department, someone crammed into a corner with boxes of what looked to me like glitter surrounding them.

They looked me up and down.

Cleo, you auld fucker, I feel you now.

They looked me up and down again, then dug their hand into one of the boxes of glitter and sprinkled it across my shoulders.

There, they said. That's you done.

I looked down at my sparkling shoulders and sighed. This was just getting worse.

Then the photoshoot began in earnest.

Aside from myself and Panti, the other members of the

cast for this new Thisispopbaby circus show at this photo-shoot were Adam Matthews (assless chaps), Megan Riordan (megaphone), Ruth Smith (violin) and Emmet Kirwan (multi-coloured shell suit). I was given a hurling helmet to complete my ensemble and we were assembled into pose after pose after increasingly unlikely and compromising pose.

There seemed to be photographers hanging from every spare vantage point: wall, ceiling or floor. It came in an unrelenting tidal wave of shutter sound and camera flash.

SnapSnapSnapSnap.

Go here. Do that.

SnapSnapSnapSnap.

Bend over this sofa. Look him in the eyes.

SnapSnapSnapSnap.

Look at the sandwich. Good. Look him in the groin. Better. Lie down between his legs. Excellent. Now look up.

SnapSnapSnapSnap.

Smoulder. Sexy. Good.

SnapSnapSnapSnap.

Pose after pose until it began to dawn on me that an awful lot of these photos seemed to be centred around my ass, or various different versions of my ass, or me peering seductively at other people's asses. Whatever way I came at it, there were an awful lot of ass shots going on around here.

After one pose that had me holding Megan above my head in a traditional strongman-type arrangement, I set her down and, just as I did, I heard another *snap* click from behind me.

I'd been doing my best to keep track of where every

photographer was at all times in an attempt to reduce my panic, in much the same way a gazelle might keep its eyes turned towards the lounging lions on the horizon. I hadn't noticed that one of them had managed to outflank me, so I got a nasty shock when I turned around to find a photographer lying on the floor, the lens of their camera centred directly between the crack of my ass.

This was almost too much. I was still technically a teacher. As far as my employer knew, I was coming back to work at Swinford Secondary School at the end of this career break, back to my job out on the cusp of the Mayo–Roscommon border. Not a place traditionally known for its bohemian attitude towards semi-nude photography and non-heteronormal sexual discourse.

If these photographs got out, then that was the end to all that. Good luck trying to face a staffroom or parent–teacher meeting with these images doing the rounds, that's to say nothing of a class full of rural adolescents with less mercy for vulnerable teachers than a Khmer Rouge death squad. I'd be done without so much as a passing comment on the matter.

I didn't even want to think about the reaction of my own family.

I found the person in charge of the photoshoot, a fellow called Tom Lawlor, and politely asked him for a word.

Tom, I began, with as much calm as my fractured resolve could muster. Where exactly are these photos going to go?

Everywhere, he said, without so much as fluttering an eyelash.

Everywhere? I repeated.

Everywhere, he confirmed.

That's just what my mate back in the theatre lobby in Letterkenny had said. It was only now that I was truly coming to understand what that meant.

Right. Cool, I said unconvincingly.

Tom caught the whiff of my indecision and tried to reassure me.

Obviously we'll send you a photo bank with all the images in there so that nothing will go out that you're not comfortable with.

This hit me like an intravenous injection of relief. Heroin couldn't have felt this good.

Oh, thank God, I said. That's wonderful news.

But …

But what?

But, well, you've got to understand that I *want* them to go everywhere.

Oh.

Yes.

Right.

Because, that's my job, you know?

Yes.

A lot of thought has gone into the arrangement here. You as the beefcake character are an important part of that. It will help to get these photos to go everywhere, which, in turn, will help us to sell the show. And it's going to be a great show.

Sure.

Tom smiled supportively at me.

So, like I said, you'll get a photo bank sent to you so you can remove any photos you really don't like. Don't worry, we won't make you do anything that you don't want to.

He gave my shoulder a friendly pat and walked off, leaving me to contemplate my fate.

He was not wrong. It wasn't like I had said no to any of this. Sure, I'd baulked at pretty much everything that had been asked of me, but I'd done all that inwardly, locked as I was in this interminable competition with myself to see how far I'd be willing to go. Which meant that, without having articulated this to *anyone* in a position of authority, and with having let the photoshoot run practically to its conclusion, it wouldn't have felt either fair or reasonable for me to turn around and suddenly say: Do you know what? I'm not comfortable with *any* of this. No. You cannot use any photos featuring my ass or my legs or my bare body in any fashion.

It wouldn't have been fair and, personally, I think I would have regretted it in the long run.

That's not to say that there weren't *some* photos that I struck out from the photo bank when it was finally sent my way. Not everything was okay, but most of it was. And that's not to say that I did not spend the next few months in abject terror at what new horror I might find myself tagged into on social media, legs akimbo and junk on show. But I'm glad that I did it.

And in the end, the lead photo chosen to promote the initial run of a show that would come to be known as *Riot* is something of which I am very, very proud. It looks class. It speaks to the core of the show and it just looks like a deadly piece of live performance, which is exactly the sort of thing I was hoping to be involved in when I started all this.

FOUR

FOOTBALL: THE EARLY YEARS

(A spud-picking talent scout, possibly truant,
and the beginnings of a career.)

In Ireland, the Gaelic Athletic Association (GAA) is more than an organisation. It's more than a dementedly bizarre calendar of fixtures. It's more than an eye-wateringly complicated system of round robins, leagues, knockouts, qualifiers and back doors. It's more than its dubious history of systematic exclusion and nationalistic flag-waving. It's more than its cash pile and its begrudging, less-than-half acceptance of the woman's side of the game. It's more than all that.

At its heart, whether it knows it or not, whether it cares about it or not, the GAA is about building community and framing identity. It does this across the country, through both codes of hurling and football (not to be confused with soccer, for any folks reading who hail from distant shores).

Coming from a rural Roscommon setting, I'd be tempted to say that it's more important for those from the country, where increasingly it's only the local club that keeps the heartbeat alive for the hundreds or thousands of struggling villages and townlands that suffer more than most from recession and emigration. Those hidden destinations that pockmark the countryside and make up the bulk of what we think of as Irish country life. Places where the pubs, post offices, shops and young people have mostly gone, leaving behind only a handful of people and the club.

But you only need to look at Dublin to see that it's not just a rural thing. It's a countrywide thing. In towns and cities, where terms like urban isolation are becoming just as real as their rural equivalent, GAA clubs still act as central hubs, places where areas such as Raheny, Ballymun, Kilmacud, St Vincent's and many others can retain a sense of themselves. The old notion of an inner-city neighbourhood might be dying, but the GAA keeps the idea of an urban community alive.

That's not to whitewash the GAA. As I've alluded to, it's a rickety construction that, in parts, is riddled with the worst kinds of conservatism and traditionalism. Both women's codes still lie outside of it, which has probably been a blessing of sorts for them, allowing them to grow and develop despite the worst efforts of the main GAA body. The distrust and fear surrounding foreign sports, while understandable, still leant itself towards a style of protectionism, casting Ireland as a utopian ideal that was completely removed from the reality of the country's situation.

I've never bought into this idea that sport and politics are separate. How can they be? Once you fly a flag, sing an anthem or wear a crest, then that sporting situation immediately becomes an expression of tribalism, whether that be on a county, provincial or national level. Tribalism is political, whether you like it or not. On a national stage, it becomes nationalism, which is what wars can be fought over. I don't understand people who cling to this belief that somehow sport is a pristine environment that remains uncontaminated by the dirty reality of politics.

And nowhere is that truer than for an organisation like the GAA, which was founded in the 1880s on the principle of promoting Gaelic games and culture against the backdrop of British rule. It's harder to get more political than that. But its politics are largely silent, bred through a performative expression of itself that is repeated annually across the country. This is what is Irish. Nothing else. This is what is masculine. Nothing else. By codifying itself in this manner, it has the effect of making the organisation seem exclusive to many people, which is such a shame when the cons of the GAA are balanced against the community-building pros of it. You only need to look at their reticence over embracing things such as the Pride flag to understand that this is an organisation that is not fully at ease with the Ireland it now finds itself in.

My life in football came to define me for the better part of two decades, from when I first picked up a ball in my primary-school days, until I finally decided to step back in my mid-to-late twenties.

Looking back now, in some way, the point at which I decided to take football seriously was almost the exact moment when the fun of football began to drain away a little for me. At one stage during secondary school, I had entirely planned my life around football. Not just in a daily or weekly fashion, but rather I had created a life plan for myself in which football would be the central component and around which everything else would orbit.

It went like this:

For my third-level education I would go to the University of Limerick. What I studied wasn't the most important thing, what mattered was that there was a good sporting culture down there and I would be able to easily travel home for matches and training as might be required. I would study to become a teacher, as that would give me the freedom to train and play as I needed to. It would mean that my summers would be completely free, which left space for me to continue to commit myself to the Fórsa Cosanta Áitiúil (FCÁ), a now-defunct version of the Irish Army Reserve. And more than anything else, it would allow me to play football.

I decided on all this in my teenage years and resolved to take the first step right away. Football would come first, and it would start now. I would train hard. I would devote myself to taking my football career as far as I possibly could. And if that meant sacrificing everything else to service it, then that's just what I would do.

There it was, my life plan. A neatly laid-out timetable that would take me right into my thirties. And after that? What? I wasn't sure, but from the vantage of my mid-teens, that didn't seem like a pressing issue.

And for the most part, that's exactly what I accomplished. I got there. I did it. I went to Limerick to study. I got myself a job as a teacher. And I played lots and lots of football, achieving, more or less, everything that was available to me.

And once I had done it, once I had gotten to this position somewhere in my mid-twenties, I suddenly realised that I couldn't shake a feeling. The 'what next' feeling. Do I just live within this structure that I've constructed for myself? Play club football until my body can no longer cope? Teach until I reach pension and retire early? Maybe do a little coaching? Get involved at the grassroots level of the game and help others do what I have done?

I could do all that. Sure. I definitely *could*. But …

Well, we'll come to all of that. But first, there was our front field.

The front field of the family farmhouse in Corrigeen, in the townland of Mantua, in the rolling county of Roscommon, was the first place where I came to know and love the whole idea of sport. When it wasn't full of marauding horses called Cleo – and sometimes when it was – that field was the cradle of our sporting development.

The field itself was big enough: a few acres of hardy Roscommon soil and thick tufts of verdant grass, running from the front of our farmhouse, down alongside the pot-holed and hedge-lined gravel track that constituted our driveway, and right up to where the local road bent itself around the perimeter of our land.

It didn't have anything in it. It was just a field. But being nothing other than a field was far from a detractor. It meant that the space was eminently flexible to whatever sport was currently the focus of our fancy. We'd spill out from the house, having watched something on telly, and immediately organise ourselves into the codes of that discipline. During the Olympics, the field became our stadium, our running track marked out by the mounds of freshly felled grass. If we'd just watched some soccer, then the field became the steep rake of the Stadio delle Alpi or acquired the indomitable grandeur of Old Trafford. And, more than anything else, after any football matches, be it league or championship, minor or senior, the field would morph into our very own Croke Park, the crisp rustle of the boundary trees providing us with our own version of cheering crowds, while we split into teams and thumped into one another as we learned the basics of the game.

Even then, in competitions arranged amongst my siblings, family or friends of close proximity, I was not considered a flair player. If we were playing soccer, I was not Ryan Giggs or Alessandro Del Piero or Ronaldinho. I had an engine; I had some strength and I was competitive. That meant that I was always, always Roy Keane.

It was just who I was. I would never escape it. Not even in football, where it would come to define me as a player.

That front field provided footballing opportunity for more than just us Bradys too. Dad was involved with training the Mantua National School team – a school which had a grand total of thirty-seven students from top to bottom. Their main pitch would frequently be unavailable for training, so often-times Dad would bring the team to our front field to train.

I was too young at the time to take part in the training itself, but I would always be out there, kicking stray balls back into the mix, and following as best I could all that was happening, replicating what moves and drills I could from my place on the edges of the session.

School matches would occur back on the main pitch, which wasn't really a pitch at all, but rather a relatively dry field – and this, within the damp and boggy landscape of Roscommon, meant that it stood out as prime athletic real estate. This field was owned by Peter Porter, who has a name I simply love, and who can still be found today driving around the country in his sky-blue cattle lorry.

Justin was my dad's name, and the team had a song they used to sing on the way to these matches. It was set to the tune of 'Put 'em Under Pressure', the Irish soccer song from the Italia '90 World Cup, and went something like this:

> *We're all part of Justin's Army,*
> *And we're all off to Porter's field,*
> *Where we'll really shake them up,*
> *When we win the schools cup,*
> *Because Mantua are the greatest football team.*

As a family, we'd generally attend these matches too, but being very young at the time we'd be prone to distraction. What made Peter Porter's field exciting from our youthful point of view was that it had a stream running along the boundary ditch which was often full of tadpoles. Whenever we got bored with the football, we'd take ourselves off to the stream to splash about and watch the wildlife.

What can I say? Country life is great.

The first pitch on which I ever actually played football was in Kilnamyrall, less than ten minutes' drive from the family home. By that stage, Mantua National School had managed to raise some funds to acquire the field opposite the local Mantua church for use as a regular pitch. This field had a fair-to-middling slope to it, so it was more like a challenging fairway than a pitch, and was also inhabited by a rather large sinkhole in one of its far corners. This sinkhole became a thing of mythologised terror amongst us young children at the time. We warned each other about the dangers of getting too near and finding ourselves dragged underground by the hungry earth forever more. It had happened before, we whispered. It could happen again.

Now, this is not how swallow holes work. They're more like turloughs, temporary rain-water lakes. But our story was more interesting, and so it stuck. However, as great as our fear of the sinkhole ever became, it was never so terrible as to prevent us from playing football. Even then, football came first.

The Mantua goalkeeper's jersey consisted of yellow and black stripes, which meant that, obviously enough, as a team we called ourselves the Bumblebees. We would play seven-a-side matches against either ourselves or other local national school teams. The team was largely comprised of the offspring of three families: the Travers, the Creggs and the Bradys, with my friend Neilus rounding things off.

There were two main methods of getting to the pitch for a match, either with Frank Creggs or with Gabe Travers.

Gabe Travers, God rest him, was a man with a pick-up truck. He had something like one of those paint-speckled, open-bed HiAce vans that any self-respecting country-based handyman would have owned at that time. He was older than my parents and came from a generation who used to send off in the post for their driver's licences, long before there was any such thing as a test. But if you were happy to risk it, he would let you pile into the back of the pick-up with as many other kids as his cringing axles could hold and he would spin you away down to the match and then maybe even drop you back home again afterwards.

If you didn't fancy that, then there was always Frank Creggs.

Frank Creggs had lost his left arm in a work accident when, as a younger man, he'd gotten himself pulled into a rock-breaking machine. But he could still drive a manual transmission, as long as there was someone in the passenger seat to work the gearstick for him. Since there were twelve Creggs children, all of whom knew how to shift a gear, this was never a significant problem, and Frank would happily drive all twelve Creggs, plus whoever else could fit into the open boot of his Toyota Camry, down to the pitch for the match, legs dangling over the moving tarmac as we sped around the curves of our familiar country lanes.

That's how we got to matches or training or anything else. As with the riding of our tractor to the community disco slightly later on in life, it was just the way things were.

At that stage, there was no gender split within the sport.

This may have been down to numbers rather than a policy of progress, but it was a great idea, nonetheless. Two of our toughest and most accomplished players were girls, and regardless of that, it was just a healthier environment to be in.

Scrabbagh were our greatest rivals of the time, and we had many a great battle with the children of that team on the sloped pitch of Kilnamyrall, titanic events that shook the bones and memories of all those who took part in or witnessed them. Those kids would later go on to play club football for Kilmore, just as we would go on to play club football with Elphin, and so the battle would continue.

This is how the local rivalries of rural Ireland are born. This is how one parish differentiates itself from another within the tapestry of townlands across a county. This is how shared histories are created, and stories about ourselves are revealed to those we hold closest. But even more than all of that, it's how communities come together. How they come to know and care for one another.

Sure thing, there's no bastard like a bastard from Scrabbagh, but that's only within the confines of the pitch. Because outside of that, there's a whole community of collaboration, volunteerism and dedication that has gone on in the background, unseen, in order to bring those two teams together on that pitch on that day, all for the privilege of trying to knock lumps out of one another.

It's a culture that, at its best, binds us together. We all get involved and we all concern ourselves with it.

For instance, the first time I was deemed old enough and

good enough to progress from the minnows of Mantua to the big leagues of Elphin went a little like this.

I was out in one of the fields back home in Corrigeen. We were planting a heap of potatoes, and myself and the rest of the brood had been sent out to do the brunt of the donkey work. Potato planting is tough work and much better suited to those with a low centre of gravity, like children. You move up and down the drill, which is the long furrow within which the potatoes will be planted, with your back bent double, sinking your hands deep into the soil to lay down halved potatoes which will act as the seedlings for a new potato plant.

As we toiled, the sound of an approaching motor caused us all to look up from our work.

Bouncing slowly up our driveway, doing its level best to navigate a lane that was more pothole than lane, was the sleek black figure of Seán Neary's BMW.

This was an impressive hunk of a vehicle. We were a farming family with only tractors and rickety people carriers to our name. That this car was the definition of slick was just an immutable fact to us. It had all the mod cons, *including* electric windows, which was the thing that excited me most.

Seán had made the trip to our farm that day to come and collect me. One of the Elphin underage teams was short a player and it had been decided that I should be brought into the squad.

In front of my family, I was called out of the field and told to wash my hands and grab my gear, before being packed into the back of this black beacon of coolness to head away and play football with the big boys.

It was a wonderful day. Like something out of a comic or a made-for-telly, Disney channel, kid's sport special.

I was even more amazed by the electric windows during the journey when, as I found myself packed into the Beamer's back seat with approximately twenty other kids bound for the game, I pushed the button to roll down my window only to discover that Seán, from his position in the driver's seat, could not only put my window up with his own special master button, but also lock it *against my will* to discourage further tampering. This was space-age stuff.

We went ahead and played the match that day, which would mark the beginning of over fifteen years of me playing for Elphin at various age levels, right up to the senior team.

What I didn't appreciate about that day until much later on was the vast network of communication that had occurred away from my sight to get me into Seán's Beamer that morning.

Seán had talked to Dad, who had consulted with Mammy, who had then gone back to Seán, who had talked to Elphin and had been chatting to the Travers and the Creggs as well. This dialogue had gone back and forth through the phone lines of the parish as they slowly figured out who was available, when they would play and how everyone would get there.

From that day onwards, I was a footballer as far as either Mantua or Elphin were concerned. I had firmly entered the fold.

A few years later, when I had grown into my teenage self, there came a moment when things got serious.

We were at something we weren't supposed to be at, out the back of the Elphin GAA pitches. I don't exactly remember what we were doing. Part of me wants to say that we were drinking on the sly, sipping cans or a bottle of Buckfast in the space behind the stand that kept you hidden from view and gave you a fair chance at escape should anyone come looking for you. Another part of me wants to tell you that we were just skiving off from school, mitching as we hung out around the pitch. In all probability, it was a bit of both. I've said before, and it is true, that I wasn't one for the underage drinking, so I could simply have been keeping the other lads company as they got themselves sauced outside of school.

Whatever it was, we had been discussing this and that, talking about life in the way you do during your adolescence, really cutting to the core of things in a fashion that all the adults around you are simply incapable of – you know, really figuring shit out.

At some stage Shane Farrell turned around to me and half-accused me with this comment. Yeah, he said. Well, it's alright for you, Ronan, you're good at football.

I don't remember exactly what was supposed to be alright for me because of football, whether it was because this gave me a purpose or an exalted position in the school, or simply meant that I was less likely to take flak if we got caught for being there, skipping school.

Either way, that comment put me back a little bit, because

until then I had never conceived of myself in those terms. Football had just been a game to me; something to do and enjoy. The comment told me that football had the potential to be more than that. It could be a purpose and direction in and of itself. It could be something to do. It could be something to aspire to.

And, apparently, I was good at it.

Prior to that, I had been able to identify other people as being the best players on the team. Other people. Not me. I'd never considered myself to be good at anything before. Sure, I was competitive, but I firmly considered myself as being similar to those around me. I'd never thought that I could aspire to a level beyond that. But behind the stands at the Elphin pitches that day, this suddenly became something that was possible.

And isn't it typically Irish that it wasn't until someone else said it to me, until someone else gave me a view of myself through their eyes, that I finally obtained the capacity to conceive of this as being a possibility. I'd been playing football for years at that point. But just for fun.

Over the following weeks and months, that thought would fester and spread into a series of questions I kept on asking myself. If I'm one of the best, where can this go? How can I improve? What's available to me? Which were then followed by another, starker realisation.

I had always looked up to those whom I thought of as the better players in our team. I looked up to them and considered them as having a responsibility to get us through games. We were on a team with them and, with their higher skill level, it was up to us to service them so they could then service the team by making sure we got a result.

If I was one of the better players, then this was a responsibility that I now had as well.

The thought was something of a shock. It made me worry that maybe I hadn't been pulling my weight so far, that I'd been too relaxed, too willing just to do what I could rather than perhaps doing what I was fully capable of.

It put an engine running in me. If I was one of the better players, then I needed to act like it.

So, I did.

FIVE

THE GREAT DISAPPEARING ACT

(Bluff, bluster and rehearsing something that isn't there.)

Fake it until you make it. That's the thing, right?

That's the conventional wisdom, anyway. That's what a lot of the books say. You know, those self-help ones with annoying photographs of people with impossibly and impeccably toothy smiles on the cover. Happy-looking fuckers who have always struck me as being more sinister than benevolent. It's that dead-behind-the-eyes stare. It makes me think that they're in a cult. Like Scientology. Or Enron. Or the ketogenic diet.

Well, look how that turned out for all of those folks. And I'm here to tell you, in no uncertain terms, that this sort of thinking can land you in big trouble.

Who knew?

When Thisispopbaby had initially approached me, it turned out that I had not been their first choice. They'd been searching for a male aerialist, preferably Irish, for a while, and their search had taken them on a Chinese-whispers-style journey of recommendations and suggestions and dead ends. Eventually they ended up talking to my friend and future circus-performance partner Aisling Ní Cheallaigh, who, in turn, put them on to me.

When they came looking for me, I was initially reluctant to engage with them, feeling myself too much of a puppy to go gambolling around with the big kids.

I'm not being awkwardly humble here. I'll quite happily tell you that *now* I'm probably the best cyr-wheel performer in the country, because I am. There's not a lot of us; best out of one you might say, but I'm still the best and that's just the truth. *Now*.

Back then I was raw as fuck. And that is also just truth.

Be honest with yourself. You'll always be better off for it.

Mostly, anyhow.

You see, and I must be frank, there is a subtle trick to understanding when you're being honest with yourself, which is helpful, and when you're simply abusing yourself, which is, obviously, not very helpful at all.

We all have a little goblin inside us. You know the one. It's that leather-skinned, pockmarked evil little bastard who perches on your shoulder and whispers all kinds of doubt and degradation into your ear whenever you're feeling low and vulnerable.

That goblin is an observant little prick too. It knows exactly what to say and when to say it to best exploit your fears, insecurities and resolve. It can puncture your ambition with one deftly placed verbal lance, because we are always and forever the biggest bullies to ourselves. The goblin knows it and feeds on it.

Honesty is acknowledging something you're not good at, and figuring out how to do it better. Self-abuse, in comparison, is when you convince yourself that not only are you shit at something, but you yourself are a piece of shit that shouldn't even bother doing anything ever, because who would ever need to hear or see anything from you?

Abuse keeps you back. Honesty pushes you forward.

So, in the spirit of honesty, honestly, I am the best cyr-wheel artist in the country, but I'm by no means perfect, and by God, I can talk myself into an awful lot of trouble sometimes.

Aisling told me to nut up and send along my stuff to Thisispopbaby when they came a-knocking because, as she rightly pointed out, the worst that could happen is that they would say no, which isn't such an awful thing at all.

That's how myself, Jenny Jennings and Philly McMahon (no, not the Dublin footballer, unless there's a remarkable double life being led by Philip, which, frankly, would be an annoyingly steroidal version of my story) from Thisispopbaby began to talk.

Our initial exchanges were over email, and they went something like this:

JennyPhilly: Hey Ronan. We're from Thisispopbaby.

This is who in the what now? I think to myself before I proceed to lie my ass off.

Ronan: Deadly. I love your work. What can I do for you?

JennyPhilly: We're looking for a male aerialist and Aisling has recommended you to us. We're making a new show for the Dublin Fringe later this year. We'd love to see some of your work. Can you send us some stuff?

Cue me furiously scrambling to gather together some

videos that make me look like anything other than the start-lingly virgin arts performer I really am.

Ronan: Sure thing. I'm primarily a wheel guy, so here's a few videos of me performing on that both on the ground and as an aerial piece. It's rough enough, but you'll get the idea.

A few days pass, during which I assume that my very obvious inexperience has scared them off and that I'm off the hook, which is mildly relieving. Until …

JennyPhilly: Those videos are great. We'll have that. What else have you got?

Okay, we're just going to have to stop things right here for a moment.

We'll have that? *We'll have that?* What did that mean? Am I hired? You haven't even told me the job or about the project or the dates (because, while I suppose that I really should know when the Dublin Fringe Festival is on, I don't).

Is this really how people are hired in the arts? Is this really how you get jobs? They've never even met me. How the fuck do they know that they'll *have that?* It's nonsense. It's like hiring a teacher based on the fact that they've seen *Dangerous Minds* and reckon that they can do a fairly mean impression of Michelle Pfeiffer.

And then. *And then* there's this 'What else have you got?'

I'll tell you what else I've got. Nothing is what. Nothing. Not a thing.

I know I'd said to them that I was *primarily* a wheel guy, but that was a lie. I had the wheel in my repertoire and that was it. I was only just getting happy with my wheel skills. I'd recently been able to get the hang of the coin-spin, something of which I was extremely proud. I'd even done a little bit of aerial wheel, where I start with my wheel suspended in the air before it descends to the floor, and I do my usual thing down there. But getting a basic grasp of the wheel had taken me the better part of three years. How on earth was I supposed to have anything else? There hadn't been *time* for anything else.

I racked my brain. Aside from the wheel, the only other piece of circus performance I could possibly lay claim to was the fact that I'd hung in a harness from a crane a few times while performing with an aerial circus crowd called Fidget Feet. I had also spent a grand total of about fifteen seconds using an apparatus known as straps. (Straps were two long, thin and strong lengths of polyester, about a palm-width across with a loop at each end, one for rigging and the other for your hand.)

Now, while I did have some videos of me performing from a crane, I really didn't think they would be able to fit a forty-metre-tall piece of heavy machinery into their production budget for this *indoor* performance. Nor did I think that anyone would have found it particularly interesting to watch me hang partially immobile from a harness while I exposed my woeful lack of flexibility, trying to strike a series of aerial dance shapes. You can get away with that forty metres off the ground with four other, far more flexible performers all around to cover you. It's not so easy to do that on your own while up on stage.

What I did have was a seven-second video clip of me

swinging in a circle on aerial straps while doing a move called a meat hook – which is about the most basic aerial manoeuvre you can imagine. This video was half of the total time I'd ever spent on the apparatus. But I decided I would send it to them anyway, half-assuming that it would convince them that, no, I didn't really have anything else.

Why I didn't just say that very thing to them, I don't really know. It shouldn't have been that hard to admit that the wheel was my only thing. Maybe part of me didn't want to scare them off with my lack of experience. In truth, being approached to perform by people I didn't know was flattering, regardless of how rinky-dink and ridiculous I suspected them to actually be.

But, more than that, I think it was that the fake it until you make it impulse can be very strong. It was just part of who I'd grown up to be. If someone asked something of you, you said yes and worried about the details afterwards. Can you work that tractor? Obviously not, but I want to get up on it so badly that I'm not going to tell you that, so yes, yes, I can work that tractor. That sort of thing.

I think that, in part, by sending along that video of me on the straps to JennyPhilly, I must simply have been acting from reflex and habit as much as from any real sense of gamesmanship or bluster. I didn't *want* to say no to anything. Let them say no for me. I'd just continue to fake it until I ran out of runway.

So I sent the straps video along.

Ronan: Well, I have begun to experiment with this piece

of apparatus called straps. Have a look at this short clip. I can look into developing something from this if you are interested?

JennyPhilly: Great. We'll have that too. Now, about this photoshoot …

They'll have that too.

Great. Just great.

I'm thrilled that they've bought my bullshit and brought me on board to this project I don't understand.

I'm not freaking out.

No.

I'm not freaking out at all.

Pause for a prolonged period of silent dread as the realisation of what consequences my actions are going to have and …

OhmyGod.

What.

Have.

I.

Done!

It's at times like this that the goblin really kicks into full gear. *You're shit, Ronan. What do you think you're playing at? Your wheel is shit anyway and now you're trying to palm off this straps bollocks on them. You're only going to embarrass yourself. You're nothing but a stupid lump of a bogman from Roscommon anyway. What are you doing amongst all these weird fucking arty fuckers? Shut up and stop fooling yourself. Go back to your farm. Go back to your school. Go back and stop making a holy living show of yourself and save everyone the pain of having to find all this out later. Just go!*

That was the self-abuse side of me. It was loud. It was vigorous. And it was emphatic. And while I couldn't quite turn it off, I had learned how to put it aside, which allowed the honest side of me to begin to talk.

The honest side of me knew that I had to figure out how to do some work in straps and I had to do it quick.

Abuse keeps you back. Honesty pushes you forward.

Forward I went.

I'd never been through a standard creation or rehearsal process before. Anything I'd done up until this point, be it any of my own short solo acts or those crane performances I mentioned, had all been done very much on the hoof. It had been done in brief, pressurised periods of time whereby you might only have a day or a few days to figure something out.

That way of working was very much a consequence of the style of outdoor, aerial circus performances I regularly found myself in, where the show generally took place in a public place with limited availability and a strict budget, which typically precluded anything so fanciful as long rehearsal periods and prolonged on-site access.

'Circus, Street Art and Spectacle', as it's officially termed by the Arts Council of Ireland, is still a very niche collection of art forms in this country, with very limited funding opportunities. This is further complicated by the fact that aerial circus and medium-to-large-scale spectacle are very expensive endeavours, occurring in a country with a very limited market space. This means that budgets are tight, and timelines are stressfully packed into near-impossibly short windows of time.

Taking this into consideration, the quality of work produced in this area is phenomenally good. This is principally down to the dedication, experience and craft of the small group of artists who make up the sector's most skilled and senior professionals. These are people who regularly repeat the loaves and fish miracle of creating huge things from practically nothing at all.

JennyPhilly from Thisispopbaby were coming from a theatre background and were, by Irish arts standards, exceedingly well resourced and supported. They were talking about a big ensemble piece in a specially created venue dedicated to the show, which would take place as the centrepiece act of the entire festival. They were talking about bringing experienced artists together into a rehearsal room over weeks, *weeks*, not days like I was used to, for a long creation and development period in order to figure out the show and get it on its feet.

Weeks is a very long time to hide that you don't actually know what you're doing, which wasn't a lie because I'd never done anything like this before, and I found the idea of all of it to be very intimidating.

What if I got up there in front of everyone to rehearse these straps that I couldn't use properly anyway and was inevitably shit? Would they kick me out of the show altogether? Would I embarrass myself in front of professional artists and tar myself with a reputation as a talentless spoofer, scuppering my performing career before it had even begun?

A meeting between Philly, Deirdre Molloy – the company manager – and myself had been organised for Dublin after the photoshoot so we could all talk properly about the project. I decided that the only thing for it was for me to come clean about everything.

We all sat down together in a quay-front café. Philly took the lead and started talking through the general idea of the show; that it would be a cabaret-style performance with different acts all linked together under the theme of a social, political, party-riot type atmosphere, busting stereotypes and being generally provocative. They wanted it to be fun and colourful and moving and hilarious. They liked my videos and they wanted me to be a part of the project.

At that point in the conversation, the space opened up for me to talk, which is where I spilled my guts to them in their entirety.

Look, I said. I'm from Roscommon. I used to be a secondary-school teacher. I'm on a career break and I'm only new to this performing thing. I'm not really a professional artist yet. I've taken a chance on this because I'm trying to become one. I haven't been in shows before. I've never done a proper rehearsal or creation period before. And those videos I sent you. I only did that because I thought you'd only want one thing. I didn't think you'd be looking for lots of things. So, I sent them along thinking you'd pick one. You see, I can genuinely do the wheel. That's grand. I've got that. No bother. But those straps. I don't know them at all. I could figure something out, but I'd have to come up with stuff from scratch and I'd need time to train and develop them for you. So, what I need from you is a decision. What do you want?

Do you want the straps, or do you want the wheel? Because I don't think I can give you both.

A small silence descended over the table as Philly and Dee tried to assimilate all the information I'd just garbled at them.

Ronan, Philly asked. How are you feeling about all of this?

Petrified, I replied truthfully.

Good, said Philly. Because we're all petrified. We're all taking a chance on this. So, let's take that chance together. How does that sound?

Relief is a wave. Have you ever noticed that? It sweeps upwards through you from the soles of your feet. Right then, at that café table, relief filled my body from the ground up, picking me up onto its crest and making me feel floaty and light.

That sounds great, Philly, I said. That sounds really great.

Good, said Philly. And don't worry. We'll figure it all out.

The meeting concluded with a commitment that the JennyPhilly duo would come down to see me in Limerick at the Irish Aerial Creation Centre where I could show them what I had, and we could take things from there.

I left that meeting feeling fantastic.

This feeling lasted a long time, right up until a few days before they were due to come and meet me in Limerick. Ahead of that, still feeling tops, I decided to send Dee Molloy a follow-up email to clarify, based on our previous meeting. Did they know which of the apparatus types they wanted as I would like to get training and prepare some stuff ahead of their visit?

Dee forwarded this onto Philly, who then replied:

Philly: Hey, Ronan. We'll still have them all. Straps and wheel, and that aerial wheel thing too. We'll see you down in Limerick. Looking forward to it.

This news sent me straight back into my dread spiral.

They had obviously completely and wilfully misunderstood what I had been trying to tell them. I couldn't give them all of it. *I didn't know how!*

Upon reflection, I think I had made a fatal assumption when Philly had offered that we all be petrified together: I had assumed that he had understood my self-inflicted anxiety and given me a reprieve. That was not the case. What he had meant was that it was okay to not know anything. Everyone was figuring things out as they went. In that, me not knowing straps would be no different to anything else in the show, so I might as well do it anyway.

That's what he'd meant. But that's not what I had understood. And once again, I began to panic.

Our Limerick date was in a few days and I had prepared nothing that wasn't my wheel. My panic froze me into a position of immobility. It's that feeling when something becomes so overwhelming that instead of doing something, doing anything to attempt to overcome it, you shut down and do nothing, pretending that perhaps it isn't there or that, if you ignore it hard enough, it will simply go away and leave you alone.

Unsurprisingly, it didn't go away, and once my freeze cracked and thawed back into panic, I went and asked Aisling for help.

Finding places to train for aerial in Ireland is not easy. The type of circus I do is relatively new to this country and there aren't the customised spaces that exist for things like music, dance and theatre. For aerial circus you need lots of height, lots of space, lots of gear and, preferably, lots of warmth to be able to do it effectively and safely. And I don't say warmth out of any sense of delicateness. If you're too cold, your muscles don't flex and move and grip like they should. They move more slowly and grip lighter, which is obviously very dangerous when you're hanging from a height supported by nothing other than your own strength.

Most aerial training spaces in this country are crammed into pre-existing buildings that aren't custom-designed to fit the demands of aerial circus and are run by people who have to make the best of what little resources they have available to them. It's not an ideal situation, but it's one common to most circus arts in Ireland.

The Irish Aerial Creation Centre is one of the few spaces in Ireland solely dedicated to aerial arts, and it is by far the biggest and best-resourced of the small number of spaces in existence. Even at that, it still lives on an old business park of tall, dark-bricked warehouse units that have been retrofitted into a sports and leisure hub.

It was founded in 2013(ish) by Chantal McCormick, a one-woman-tornado of a human being who has been central to a lot of what has made Irish aerial arts what they are today, and is certainly one of the prime reasons why I am where I am.

Her company, the aforementioned Fidget Feet, who very kindly hung me from cranes and organised events such as the Irish Aerial Dance Fest in Donegal where I had my pre-photoshoot meltdown, were in residence in the centre and regularly ran professional and creative development courses for people like myself and Aisling.

So, by the luck of the calendar, we happened to be down at the Creation Centre doing one of these courses, which would then lead me into this meeting with JennyPhilly about *Riot*.

In between one of the gaps in this course, Aisling took me aside. She had never used straps before either, but she had used fabric and she said that they were similar-ish. They were both two lengths of material rigged from the same point in the ceiling. She would show me what moves she knew for fabric, then I could try them on straps. From there, we could see what worked and what didn't.

It sounded like a plan to me, and it was sure as hell a lot better than anything else I had in mind. Over the course of thirty minutes, Aisling showed me what she knew. I then parroted that back to her on the straps, and that was that. Anything I knew I would show to JennyPhilly. Everything else would just have to wait. As it turned out, what I learned in those thirty minutes formed the basis of my aerial straps act for the initial run of *Riot* at the Fringe Festival.

JennyPhilly came to the Creation Centre and I showed them what I had, rough as fuck as it was. They nodded and smiled, not really telling me much about what they thought or feared.

Aisling and JennyPhilly didn't know one another, but Aisling was there for this showing of my newfound skills on straps as I needed someone to counterweight me (lift me in the air via a pully system, which required every ounce of strength Aisling could muster since I am roughly twice her weight). She was also there, of course, because I was desperate for moral support. Aisling came through on both counts.

Now, maybe Aisling was providing conversational cover for my evident deficiency on the straps, or perhaps she was talking to provide distraction so JennyPhilly didn't get second thoughts about bringing me on board for *Riot* – I mean, I had officially been hired for the show, but I didn't know how official that really was. I'd heard of other performers getting axed during rehearsals, or at the last minute before a premiere even, and so I wasn't at all confident that – based on what I was showing them now – they wouldn't just decide to cut their losses and move on without me. Whatever it was, somehow, at some point during her conversations with JennyPhilly, she managed to make reference to my previous life as an inter-county footballer with Roscommon. I hadn't mentioned it before, neither in my emails nor in my confessional diatribe in that quay-front café in Dublin, so this came as news to both of them.

Upon hearing it, and as one, JennyPhilly stopped and looked around at Aisling.

Say what? they said.

He used to play for Roscommon, she repeated.

Play?

Yeah.

Like on a field. With a ball.

Sure.

With other men?

Think so. I don't watch much sports myself.

For the GAA?

You have me doubting myself now. Hang on a sec. Ronan!

Yeah, I replied.

You used to play football, didn't you? I'm getting that right, aren't I?

Sure did. Club with Elphin. Inter-county with Roscommon. Won the Connacht title and all.

JennyPhilly sat back with a dazed, happy look in their eyes. This was more than they could have ever hoped for. In that instant, a whole new aspect of the show they were planning opened up to them.

I have no way of knowing to what extent my skills or my football history sold them on my position as an integral part of what they were planning. What I do know is that from there, things began to unfold quite rapidly.

Following the Creation Centre, I began to receive emails from JennyPhilly about ideas they had for my character in the show. They wanted to present something that was gender-fluid, something that would challenge the traditional concepts of what it was to be male or female or anything in between within an Irish context.

They sent me videos of this beautifully androgynous man, long-haired and long-limbed, doing these incredibly feminine dance moves through a farmyard. They wanted something similar for me. They wanted to double down on my history in the GAA as a basis for the character I was to play, and then confuse and confront that with an uber-sexualised, hyper-feminine striptease.

It might come as a surprise, but it wasn't the striptease element of this idea I had a problem with. I'd been messing around with something like that as a comedy sketch back up in Donegal at the Irish Aerial Dance Fest. That was okay, I could get behind that. It was the graceful femininity they were asking me to pull off that was the challenge. I was a clunky, brick of a bogman from Roscommon. I didn't come with flexibility and grace built into me. I just didn't have it. I had nothing to go on. I didn't know that world. And I wasn't sure that I could pull it off in the way that they wanted me to.

But that was the idea. JennyPhilly were firm on it. And I was eager to please. So that's the direction we brought with us into the rehearsal room.

***

Our rehearsal room was a community centre in Drimnagh. One of those local amenities that double up as places for night classes and community groups and, on election days, polling stations. These places are great for making theatre because they are roughly city-central and relatively cheap. For aerial, however, they are almost entirely useless as they have nowhere and nothing to rig from.

This meant that for almost the entire run of our initial

rehearsal period in Dublin in those summer months of 2016, leading up to the show's premiere at the Dublin Fringe Festival in late August, I was unable to properly rehearse my act. While the other performers were doing their bits at full pelt, getting notes and honing the details, I was confined to marking things out, walking around in a circle while pretending that I was in the air, pulling a move and looking sexy (I hoped).

My inexperience at that time meant that I couldn't count music the way other performers can. Instead I had to mark out parts of the song so I would know that at a certain chorus or a particular bridge I was meant to be in a certain place and move in a particular way at that stage of my routine. If I wasn't at my mark, then something had gone wrong. It made for a strange and weirdly disheartening experience, but I was used to toughing it out. Fake it until you make it. So that's what I did.

None of this did anything for my confidence, however. Especially as I watched the other acts just get better and better while I continued to walk in a stolid circle at half-pace, pretending to be hanging from the ceiling. More than ever, I felt I was play-acting at what these other people were doing for real.

This was further compounded when every so often JennyPhilly would pipe up with a request that I, 'Do it again but sexier this time. You know, channel your inner stripper. Your inner queen.'

They still didn't understand that I didn't know how. I was a lump of an Irish man. We are not renowned for our suave and collected sexiness. Colin Farrell, maybe? Pierce Brosnan at a push. But even at that, I'm not sure we pull it off very well. Still, I tried my best, afraid all the while that I was failing badly.

This lack of rigging meant that we had to timetable 'away days' into the rehearsal schedule for just myself and Jenny (subtracted from Philly this time) to head over to the Taking Flight aerial and acrobatics studio, who were based in The Chocolate Factory at the time, to get some real development on my acts done. These days would be split into two sessions. In the morning we would focus on my straps piece. Then, in the afternoon we would run through my aerial wheel act.

In the theatre, the way things work is that the performers run a piece, then the director gives notes, the performers learn from those notes, and then the piece is run again. In this way things are developed through a continuous cycle of repetition and gradual improvement. Jenny lived and breathed the theatre, and it was only natural for her to bring this method through into working with a circus act. I was young, inexperienced and, like a dolefully persistent child attempting to impress a disinterested parent, I was desperate to give Jenny what she asked for.

In that vein, this is what would happen:

We would meet at the training space, talk for a bit, I'd warm up, then we'd talk a bit more, then we'd do a run of the straps piece, after which Jenny would give notes, I'd listen to the notes, then I would go and do another run … and things would get worse.

Wash. Rinse. Repeat.

Every time we did it. Every time she gave notes. Every time it got worse.

After the last run of the morning straps session, this phenomenon could no longer go uncommented on.

I'm just not sure you're getting what I'm saying, Jenny said.

I nodded, not because I agreed, but because I was too bollocksed to say anything. We'd run the act over and over and over, and all I wanted to do was slump into a corner of the training studio and press some food into my face.

We broke for lunch and then came back afterwards to work on the aerial wheel act.

The wheel was what I was supposed to be good at. I'd told them that the wheel was no bother. I had this one *in the bag*. That's what I'd led them to believe.

But exactly the same thing happened. We'd run it. Jenny would give notes. Things would get worse.

We got halfway through the afternoon session and Jenny stopped things once again.

You know, I think things are actually getting worse, she said.

I was now too tired to let my inexperience and my need to please get in the way of what I really thought.

No shit, Jenny, I said. I'm completely knackered over here.

How do you mean? she asked.

I mean, doing all of this stuff is hard work. I feel like I've been doing back-to-back CrossFit sessions here. I'm fucked.

How fucked?

I've basically got jelly arms over here.

Well, how do you normally do it?

I don't *know*, Jenny. That's what I've been trying to tell ye. Since the start. I've never done this before. I don't know how you normally do it.

I see, she replied. That's interesting. Do … do you want to take a rest?

Oh, thank God.

From there, things began to improve.

If I'd been more experienced, I would have been able to communicate this to Jenny at the very beginning, but my rookie status meant that I'd tried to do what I would have done on the training pitch or in the gym – just put my head down and bull-headedly power through anything that was difficult. Break it down by force was my general approach to life, and I didn't have the wherewithal to understand that I couldn't do that here. That I needed to look after myself in order to be worth a damn to anyone.

Jenny, for her part, simply didn't know that this was the case for hyper-physical performing types like circus, and so she couldn't lend her experience to me there. But she learned fast, and it quickly became understood that there were only limited returns to be gained from running my acts back to back to back, and that, as counter-intuitive as it might have sounded, you'd get a lot more from me if you let me have a twenty-minute snooze in the corner than you would by driving me into a mountainside time and time again.

Sports conditioning coaches would have been able to tell

you all about this. Most professional (and most GAA) athletes know the importance of naps for recovery and performance. But for some reason I never thought of it in those terms until I'd gone through the lived experience of failing at it the other way. Which is just the story of life, I suppose. We can be told something until the cows are home, fed, watered and fast asleep, but until we actually do something for ourselves, we won't understand it.

The *Riot* rehearsals became a learning curve for both myself and the Thisispopbaby team, as they pushed themselves out of the theatre world and into the circus world, while I pushed myself out of my old mentality and into a more artistic one, where communication was always key. Unless you told someone what you were feeling, they had no way of knowing it. It was a simple concept, but it went against every grain of the old Irish way within which I had grown up. It was like correcting your physical posture – if you didn't think about it constantly, then, before you knew it, you had reverted back to the old stooped and crooked version of yourself. I had to remind myself to talk, to share, regardless of whether or not I felt that I might say something stupid. I had to communicate, regardless of whether or not the goblin might just want me to shut up.

It was a revealing experience, and one that let me grow in ways that would help me over both the course of *Riot* and my own work beyond that.

It was also revealing to be experiencing the creation of a show from a theatre point of view rather than a circus one.

As I said, Thisispopbaby were unbelievably well resourced compared to a circus company. That isn't to say that they had lots of money to waste and fritter. They didn't. Every penny was made to count. But, comparatively speaking, they were rich when you came in from a circus context.

The simple truth of the matter is that there is more money and more opportunity available for you in Ireland when you come from a theatre background. I had been used to working manic, full-on, short projects, where there were no such things as lunch breaks and 5 p.m. wrap times, because you might only have less than twenty-four hours to get a performance set up, rehearsed, performed and packed away.

While working for Fidget Feet, who do the work of six companies on the budget of less than one, we would frequently have to park a crane, mark out our performance area, help with the rigging, do a few run-throughs, lay out the costumes, get ourselves warmed up, do our own make-up, perform the show or shows, then do everything in reverse, packing and de-rigging everything until we were back in our van or cars and on our way back home. It didn't matter if you were a performer or a director or anything in between. Everyone pitched in.

That is not a situation that is peculiar to Fidget Feet either. That's just the circus way. Everyone does everything. It's how the traditional circuses do it, and it's how most of the contemporary, spectacle and street-art people do it too. What other choice do they have? They can't afford anything else.

But with Thisispopbaby there were people to do things for you. There were stage managers and costume designers and make-up artists. We would start in the morning at a reasonable time. We would have a small break *and* a lunch break. We would finish by five and everyone would go home. If JennyPhilly needed something, they would ask the person responsible to get it done. The performers were there to perform. Nothing else. It was just weird for me. I'd come into this prepared for a marathon sprint, but we were only working at a jog.

And none of this is criticism. It was a lovely, lovely change of pace. It made the rehearsals a space for me to learn and develop in a way that was entirely unfamiliar to me, and ultimately extremely beneficial. But I'd be lying if I didn't admit that I just wish the rest of the Irish circus sector had the opportunity to do things this way too.

***

Rehearsal rolled along, bit by bit the show came together, and sooner than expected, our premiere performances at the Dublin Fringe Festival were upon us.

There's a funny thing about making a show. Generally speaking, you do so in total isolation from an audience. Not always, but mostly. Within the rehearsal room the only people watching it are either your fellow performers, who have already seen it more times than they care to count and who are probably just bored, or people who are there in a creative capacity and whose job it is to give constructive criticism. It means that after every run you are given a slew of notes and directions, areas to improve and things to remember, which is all necessary and vital to make the show ready, but has the unavoidable consequence of removing the fun from the performance and putting everyone involved into a position where they have no honest idea whether or not what they are making is any good.

At all.

You fly by your instincts on what you think might be good, but until you get it in front of an audience, you really just don't know.

That's where we were at with *Riot*. And we were petrified.

On paper, this show should not have worked. On paper it was a bunch of theatre folk turning their hand towards a circus cabaret, which wasn't what they knew or understood. On paper it was a bunch of disjointed and, in some cases, purely aspirational acts linked together by a set of almost intangible themes. There was easily a chance that it would be a muddled mess, and that we'd end up managing to say nothing very much at all.

On paper it should have been a disaster, and as the premiere began to loom at us from over our shoulders, we really began to wonder if what we had produced was actually any good.

And what was worse was the buzz that surrounded the show was intensifying at an alarming rate. We were the centrepiece of the festival and we were telling people, and urging people to tell others, that this show was going to be something special. But none of us were really sure that this was anything like the case.

We were a mass of nerves and fears, trying our best to keep

each other from creating a despair feedback loop that might sink us all.

And then there was my act and my nerves and my insecurities on top of all of that.

I'd gotten to a point where I was actively *not* telling certain people about the show. There were some whom I couldn't avoid telling, such as my girlfriend Michelle (obviously) and my family and some of my very close circus colleagues like Aisling. But the people who didn't know – the people from back home or from university or the school staffroom, and definitely, definitely, *definitely* the lads from the football team – these were people I avoided telling. I couldn't. I couldn't bring myself to risk a fall like that. Fine, I'd managed to beat the goblin. I'd gone through with it when I'd given myself multiple opportunities to back out. But I just couldn't open out the show to everyone in case it was a total disaster. I couldn't face the embarrassment of everyone knowing what a tit I'd potentially made of myself.

In that area, the goblin definitely won. And he did so because, while everyone else was freaking out about the show in its totality, I was primarily focused on my own particular role within it.

In my head, I was fully sure that everyone else's part in the show was great, and that it was only my part that would let the whole thing down. Many times I had entertained the nightmare scenario of the show tanking solely thanks to my clunky and toe-curling ineptitude. As the premiere drew close, it repeated in my mind over and over.

For my aerial-hoop act they had put me into a pink-and-blue leotard that made me look just like those drumstick lollipops you used to get as a child. You know those chewy feckers that would just pull the fillings right out of your head. I looked like that. Which made it hard to take myself seriously.

For that piece we were using some extracts from the writings of Michael Harding, which he had kindly recorded for the show. It was about his time in the priesthood and his experience of growing old. It was just a lovely story told in this unique way that Michael has of making the ordinary become fascinating, sad and nostalgic and very, very human. His voice-over wove around the movement and music in my act, and here I was dressed like a drumstick, prancing about and shitting all over it. I soon introduced a new addendum into my nightmare scenarios – the post-show fantasy of Michael making a beeline for me in an absolute rage, where he would spew and froth at the mockery that we, no, that *I* had made of his tender piece of writing.

And then there was the aerial-straps striptease. We'd ended up making the choice of dressing me up in full GAA football gear, from which, and with the aid of a few packets of Tayto crisps to shower over the imagined crowds, I would strip right down into something very similar to the pink underwear I'd been forced into for the photoshoot.

Suffice it to say that I was awash with worry. Part of me was even concerned that I might get sued by the GAA for desecrating the Roscommon inter-county jersey. I was attacking myself from all angles, the goblin in overdrive.

We were performing in a specially erected spiegeltent situated in Merrion Square. It was a fantastic, German-style, low-light and almost Gothic-feeling cabaret tent that could accommodate a few hundred people. We were the main attraction, and in the days leading up to the opening, we moved in. The days quickly passed in the weird and furious calm of pre-premiere preparations.

My anxiety only grew.

Merrion Square is right beside the Holles Street Maternity Hospital. To ease the tension, we began to joke about how many babies had now been born to the soundtrack of our rehearsals, but deep down I was harbouring a jealousy for those newborns. How comfortable and how cared for they must be. How safe from expectation they were, at least for now. How I wished that I too could swaddle up my fragile confidence in warm blankets and just go to sleep and wait until this whole thing had blown over.

Prior to our first public preview, we did a special, warm-up showing for the Fringe Festival staff. It would be the first time that we'd get any sense of what we had made – whether it was any good or if we'd be staring down the barrel of performing a turkey in front of ever-diminishing crowds over the duration of the festival.

What we were presenting was a little bit out there; a circus cabaret of different acts celebrating queer culture, women's rights and variously poking fun (in a half-serious manner) at some of the areas in which Ireland still needed to progress as a society. It incorporated a variety of comedic dance, circus, music and clowning acts that were interspersed between sections of rebellious spoken word and rousing guest speeches. All of this was joined together through the skill and charisma of Panti Bliss, who acted as the show's ringmaster and the creative prism through which everything else was funnelled.

Like I said, it was out there. And as we waited for the festival staff to arrive for the special warm-up performance, the full force of precisely how out there it was grabbed hold of the entire cast. Each and every one of us was a messy puddle of nerves, made worse by the knowledge that it was too late now to do anything about it. We could only perform what we'd made and hope for the best.

The festival staff shuffled in ahead of the showing and dutifully took their seats around the runway that jutted out into the middle of the audience from the main stage at one end of the tent. There were a few dozen of them. A polite and hopefully friendly audience.

The lights went down.

And we blew the roof off the place.

Shortly after that, the first preview audience arrived and took their places. We had a full house. The pleasantly anticipatory hum of pre-show chatter drifted from the main arena and into the backstage area where we all got ourselves prepared. Once again, the lights went down.

And we blew the roof off the place. Again.

How to explain the feeling after a successful opening performance? It's a strange concoction of manic relief and adrenaline-fuelled euphoria. Every part of your body is tingling, like you are at the peak of your human capacity, like you could almost break free of the Earth's gravity and go floating off through the atmosphere … almost. Because beneath it all is a weak-kneed exhaustion. All your energy has been spent in pulling this thing off and, what's more, you know that this is only the beginning.

You can never replicate the energy of an audience in a rehearsal room. It's a physical sensation that beams directly from the crowd to you on stage. You feed from it and they in turn react to you, and in that way it grows and grows to almost a fever pitch. You can never anticipate exactly how enthusiastic they have the capacity to become. You don't even know the areas where they are going to find enjoyment, because, without fail, an engaged audience will always, always, always find stuff entertaining that you had never even considered could be anything other than a procedural element of the show. They laugh or gasp or applaud, and that becomes part of the show. Only when the audience are there can you truly begin to understand what the show is and what it might become. Things are never finished in the rehearsal room. They are not meant to be. They need to get out in front of people in order to grow and evolve and continue.

And what's more, when you find yourself in front of an eager crowd, you suddenly remember that things are fun. These acts, over which I had dug myself into an ever-deepening hole, were fun. They were comedic and tender and provocative. I didn't need to be fearful of this audience, because they were into it. They got it in a way I hadn't up until we all gathered in the same place to share this experience together.

That's the magic of performing for people, both as an audience member and a performer – and we all are a little of both. When it's good, it's a shared experience that lifts everyone participating onto another level. I'm not getting self-important. It's not that it's life-changing exactly. But it does have an effect. You can get this at sporting events as well. The shared sense of euphoria after a dramatic game. The feeling that something special has occurred, that life, in its way, has briefly and wonderfully been pushed to its limits. It's something that you taste. It's something that you take away with you. And it's something that a part of you never forgets.

I've never forgotten that feeling from *Riot*. And it was to become a fire in me to find out what else I might be able to accomplish.

For the rest of the first run at the Fringe Festival, dear old Dublin town went nuts. We sold out from end to end. You couldn't have pried tickets loose from the rigor-mortised grip of the dead. We were inundated with press requests, of which I became one of the focal points, the GAA star that ran away with the circus. I was in print, radio and broadcast. I needn't have worried about not telling people – they were going to find out anyway. And it was a good story to tell.

Sure, aren't I still telling it to you now?

However, above everything else, my absolute highlight of that first run was Michael Harding. The man I had come to dread, having searched the web for his image and come across the profile picture used for his byline in *The Irish Times*, which cast him as a very serious and potentially dour individual, came to see the show. Much like my nightmare fantasy, he did indeed make a beeline for me after the performance. This man from Cavan, of whom I'd been so fearful, so afraid that he'd think I'd abused his work, came over and said it was great.

That helped me understand a lot.

It made me realise that while I had reluctantly agreed to be in a show that was steeped in queer culture, I still didn't quite get it, and through that sense of being uncomfortable and ill at ease, I had begun to imprint my own concerns upon other people, people I didn't know and people I did.

I resolved to learn from that.

And it was okay if I was only beginning to get to grips with queer culture, because my journey with *Riot* was only beginning.

SIX

FOOTBALL: MAKING COUNTY

(Micro-focused out of fun and the finer points of obsession.)

Looking back on the years I devoted to football is a strange experience.

It's not that it's an uncomfortable sensation. Quite the opposite. I am extremely proud of my footballing achievements. Which is not to say that I don't have the odd regret, because I do. No. It's not strange because of discomfort. It's strange because there's so little I do genuinely remember that well at all.

The ten-or-so-year period, beginning in my mid-teens, which was when I decided to start taking football seriously, through to my mid-twenties, where I began to slowly move away from it, is a congealed blur; confused fragments that do not seem substantive enough to cover the sheer tonnage of time and effort I put into this portion of my life.

There are other people, people I know well and like even more, who have played on teams with me and who possess an encyclopaedic recall for every match they've ever played, every training session they ever did. They can tell you who we played, what the score was, who scored, who came on, what we did before the match, where we went after. They can run through it like they're reading from an internal sporting ledger.

I cannot do the same.

There is, I think, a reason for this. And it comes down to the mentality I employed as a footballer throughout my career. Once I'd decided to devote myself to the sport, everything I did became about how I could maximise my improvement, how I could deliver the best efficiency for the effort I expended, how I could quickly keep moving from one thing to the next, always chasing, always progressing.

It made me insatiable for small gains. I bent my being around football. It was placed above and beyond everything else. I became militant about how I approached it. And, as such, I turned every day, every step, every session and match, into a clone of itself, an endlessly repeating sequence built around the hopes of achieving some vague and ill-defined promised land at the end of it all.

By being ever forward-facing in my mentality, I drained the tens of thousands of hours I put into football of their emotional core, classifying most of it as disposable, which made it next to impossible for me to form meaningful memories around that time. It was all so disconnected from the present tense, sacrificed instead for the prospect of the future.

I don't mean to say that I remember *nothing*. That's not true. I do remember things. But the effort involved in sorting one instance from the next is very difficult, and in some cases, there are moments and memories I have lost for good.

Which is a shame, because I loved my time playing football. I revelled in its competition. I excelled in its structure. And I committed to its goals.

For most young, decently competitive footballers, this goal is centred around the idea of 'making county'. Making county is the pinnacle. It's what the whole process is for. If you make county, then you have made *it*.

You get it fed to you from the earliest of ages. Watching it on telly, or kicking around with a ball in the field, you have the adults and older kids around you telling you that the lads who make county are great lads. They are pointed out to you as people to aspire to. *Would you like to play county when you're older? Would you like to be like him?* Those are the questions that get repeated to you time and time again. And as a kid you agree. Why wouldn't you? You *would* like to be like those lads. It seems like such a glamorous and mythical existence. These people are heroes, taking proudly to the field to engage in the noblest of sporting pursuits and the greatest of Irish traditions.

Yes. I *would* like to make county, you begin to say to yourself. And pretty soon it becomes natural to want it. Sure, isn't it all you ever wanted? The idea that there might have been a time before this point, where this feeling was not the case, diminishes and then disappears against the sheer force of everyone's insistence.

For me, I'm sure that there was a time when I wasn't particularly concerned about making county, a brief period in my early youth where football did not dominate my aspirations. There must have been. But I don't remember it, so it might as well not exist.

That's how mentalities and assumptions and biases and traditions and attitudes are born. They are repeated to you from every angle until their utterance doesn't seem like an utterance at all. It is instead just common knowledge – a belief shared by everyone that things have always been like this. Which makes it very hard to comprehend it ever being different. This is what has helped create such an elevated platform for the GAA in general and the inter-county competition in particular.

Change has come to this country, in things like divorce, women's rights, gay rights and a whole swathe of more subtle social progressions, but it has come slowly and has been hard-fought for by people who are not like me. In many ways, change has come in spite of people like me. And I am so thankful for the hard work of those people who fought for things the importance of which I did not understand until after they had been implemented. Long may it endure, because without their work, I would have continued to internalise the older social norms as being natural.

As it was, making county was the model for success I internalised during my childhood. And so I devoted myself to it.

The road to making county is littered with gym sessions, foil-wrapped dinners, mud-soiled gear bags, ice packs for bangs, bruises and sprains, managerial bollockings, club matches, development squads through all age levels, missed classes, skipped homework, parental bollockings, stiff bodies, aching muscles, more matches, more training, partner bollockings and, above all, a complete devotion to making county above everything else.

There's simply no room for a life outside of it. You either want county or you don't. There is no middle ground.

This suited me and my tendency towards obsession very well. I was only too happy to jettison anything that could be considered as extra-curricular to football from my life. Good luck and good riddance, I said. If it wasn't going to help me make the senior Roscommon inter-county football squad, then I regarded it as an unhealthy distraction which needed to be dispensed with.

School was unavoidable, but my commitment to it was purely perfunctory. It had to be completed so I could progress with my plan to go to college and become a teacher, which would then, in turn, optimise my potential as a career footballer.

The flaws here should be obvious. Football isn't a career. Bar a handful of unique exceptions, none of which come at the playing level of the game, both Gaelic football and hurling are amateur athletic pursuits that will never pay you a wage, and certainly won't set you up for life beyond the duration of your playing days.

Yes, of course, for inter-county players there is a whole world of financial perks, official expenses, off-the-books donations, courtesy cars and sponsorship opportunities, but none of that makes for a career-type salary. And yet, at an inter-county level, the sport is basically professional when you look at the training regimes and time commitment required.

It makes for a dangerous concoction. The temptation for people to sacrifice their long-term future for the short-to-mid-term highs the game provides is only too apparent. I was not particularly academically minded, but I had enough sense and foresight to understand that I would, nominally at least, need something beyond football for later life. There are plenty of others like me too. But there are also those who struggle with that, landing themselves in difficulty once their playing days end or when things do not turn out how they planned.

This is where the much-vaunted status of being considered a footballing prospect becomes so important. Progressing from my days as a child with Mantua, to my teenage years with Elphin, I was quickly identified as a prime candidate for development. This got me selected for the various development squads that tier the ages between Under–15s, Under–16s and into Minor and Under–21, all of which leads towards county, should you make it that far.

Being part of those development squads is an intoxicating experience. I don't mean that we were out on the beer or the like (although I'm sure we occasionally were, and I'm sure that still happens a lot). I mean that being selected above other players your age in the club and league around you puts you up on a pedestal.

It's not particularly nice, and I'm not claiming that it's healthy, but it is wonderful. Through your 'own' efforts, you have managed to get yourself picked out as being a better player than the others who surround you. You come to feel a certain sense of superiority, which is all the more addictive since you can point to your selection as a justification for it. It takes a special kind of person to not have their sense of themselves swelled by that.

As I progressed through this system, some faces would come and go, as those who dropped off the pace were replaced by fresh recruits. But, by and large, the core group of players who made it onto that first development squad were the same players who progressed up the levels.

It meant that I found myself suddenly surrounded by these other players from rival clubs whom I would always have considered as being standout players and dangerous opponents in their own right. And now I was here too, with them.

Again, it was wonderful and seductive, but it was also very dangerous.

There can be an aura of entitlement that develops around particular types of people who go through this system. They grow up with the repeated experience of being minded and having all the best opportunities pushed purposefully their way. That is a process which can become perilous when someone begins to expect these things, both inside and outside of football, as their due.

It's the idea of the 'locker-room' culture that has become so exposed in recent years as a refuge of childish chauvinism. You and your boys, you are the chosen ones. You have been elevated, and you have been lauded, and you have come to expect a certain share of what's around you.

How does that manifest?

It does so in a number of different ways, but most embarrassingly and most painfully, looking back, it would have been in my attitude towards women.

Courtship in Ireland is, at the best of times, a complicated and conflicted mess of introversions, repressions and bad communication. We rely far too heavily on alcohol as a means of uninhibiting ourselves enough to actually approach and talk to people we fancy. And with a traditionalist, rural male upbringing behind you, super-charged on the perceived (and real) status that comes from being a county-development footballer, it has the effect – or at least the potential – to turn you into the most depressingly stereotypical, insistent, forceful, young adult man when it comes to courting.

So you become *that* guy, who is insistent, repetitive to the point of nagging, and definitely entitled. You approach women as a conquest, rarely doubting your appeal to them, and always thinking that you know what they want better than they do themselves.

You don't always succeed, but you are never discouraged.

I want and need to be clear. I am not talking about serious sexual crime here, although goodness knows that this way of thinking and acting can be the foundation for that in extreme circumstances. I am talking about the way certain problematic male attitudes towards women, especially within a sexual context, have been normalised and made to feel everyday – the way we as men talk about them, the objectification, the sense of entitlement.

I cringe now to think of how I acted, how uncomfortable I must have made certain women feel with the level of my persistence. I didn't understand that I was doing anything wrong. I didn't even think I was being annoying. It was just the normal way of things at the time as I had grown up to understand them. That's not an excuse, it's just a reason. Let me be unequivocal. I was wrong to act in that way – it was the worst kind of juvenile male pestering and it must have been horrible to endure for the women I inflicted it upon. That it was the norm and the tradition isn't good enough. But it is the truth.

It's how things were. I cannot change that now. Once again, I can only be thankful for the hard work of other people – my friends, my partner, my colleagues – and the broader actions of other people who have helped to change the culture in Ireland. It is they who have put me in the position to realise this.

I don't think it's a huge coincidence that I did a lot of my growing up away from football. I did it in university (to a point). I did it in my teaching career. I did it with Michelle. I did it in circus.

Not so much in football.

Sure, I could say that I learned dedication and hard work through the sport, but in actuality I think it was my pre-existing determination and work ethic that gave me a shot at football in the first place.

But there we have it. I'm no better than anyone else. Yet when I made the development squads, and was firmly on the path to making county, I felt just as entitled and self-satisfied as most of the other lads around me.

I am pretty comfortable with my ability to be honest with myself. As a footballer, this meant I had a decent understanding of what I was good at and where my shortcomings were. As I developed as a player, that understanding allowed me to make the conscious choice to accentuate my strengths and dedicate myself to maximising their potential, rather than trying to force myself into being something I was not. This wasn't about being negative or admitting defeat. It was about honesty; it was about understanding how I could be most effective and give myself the best opportunity to have a shot at the county panel.

I was always strong, with a lot of power and force, and I could couple this with a decent burst of speed. I'm not saying I could go like a hare down a track, but I was no slouch and you would never have targeted me specifically as one to be beaten for pace. In addition to that, I was innately competitive. There was a fire in me to compete that was there from birth. It ensured that, no matter the game, no matter the opponent, and no matter my frame of mind, I would always be up for the contest.

It evolved into a style of play that could best be described as controlled aggression. I was going to go into a game, and I was going to step up to whomever I was paired against. I would not allow myself to be intimidated by anything or anyone. In fact, I would actively relish the prospect of being pushed to my limits within a game.

My being considered a prominent player often meant that I would be pitted directly against the star player of the opposing team. This was exactly what I wanted. It was the pinnacle of in-game competition, and it presented me with the opportunity to prove myself as worthy, over and over and over.

Because that's the thing. You are always trying to prove yourself. At least, that's how it was for me. No matter how many Elphin teams I starred in, or how many county-development panels I was selected for, I always wanted to show that I belonged there.

In games this would turn into a cat-and-mouse scenario between me and my mark. Generally speaking, I had enough about me to win nearly every ball that might come my direction. I had the toolkit to either win it outright or disrupt things enough to cause breaking ball, which I would then have the strength and speed to recover. And while this was satisfying, it wasn't always enough. Sometimes I would have to go further, to show just how dominant I was, to send a message.

This would mean letting a ball come to my opponent, allowing them enough time to gather possession but not enough to get themselves set, timing it just right so that I came in and challenged for the ball as hard as I could. I wanted to lay them out. I wanted to put them on the ground so they knew exactly how deep in my pocket they were.

All legal. I would only ever challenge within the rules of the game. But I would step right the way up to the line of what was allowed. I would take it just far enough to still be okay.

Why?

This sounds brutal to say and feels even worse to write, but the satisfaction of permissible violence is undeniably alluring. The knowledge that you are allowed to do it, that you are operating within an agreed set of rules and circumstances. But it's the sensation of making yourself physically dominant that is the drug. It's the same thinking that makes a heavy hit in American football, or a hefty tackle in rugby, or a full-blooded round of boxing, so innately satisfying. It's two evenly enough matched opponents stepping up to one another and seeing who can best whom.

It wasn't about *wanting* to hurt anyone. That was never the aim. Or never my aim. I never set out to injure an opponent. But the pitch was a battlefield with rules that every player agreed to. And for the duration of the game, the battle was on. It was exhilarating to find yourself in the midst of that tit-for-tat struggle. If you got hit and put on your arse, then could you get up and hit back and put the other guy down? Could you give as good as you got? How far could you take this? How far could you stick it out?

And then, once the game was over, you all shook hands. Everything that just happened could be forgotten. You'd wish your opponent well and hope that maybe, someday, ye'd be able to do it all again.

Ultimately, the thrill of physical contest has nothing to do with the person you're playing against. Not really. It's an internal test. It's about seeing how far *you* can go. Limits are invisible and forever shifting. It means that you are continually in a process of revealing where they lie, of walking right up to them and seeing if, today, they can be pushed a little bit further, or if, today, they're going to push you back.

Every contest is a discovery of yourself. The other player or the other team are really little more than a means of facilitating this, a tool to help you better know yourself.

That's why it wasn't about hurting anybody. Yes, the thrill of violence was and is a real thing. And it was seductive. But this thrill wasn't derived from the inflicting of pain, it was born from a testing of strength.

This is also why – for me, at least – the goings-on in a match never spilled off the field and into normal life. I never went away carrying a grudge or harbouring a vendetta. If someone caught me with a dirty one on the pitch, then that was just the way of the game. I knew the risks going in, we all did, so that was okay.

There were other people who weren't able to do that. They'd get a dig or a kick or a box during a game, which would turn into an internal scar they would carry with them, an unfolding anger that would later reveal itself, perhaps in a fight at a social occasion during some night out on the town, with one lad charging at another from across a dark and noisy dance floor.

I never did that. This sort of thinking came to define me as a player. Just as I was always Roy Keane when I played soccer as a young lad, I was always the guy who would never stop and never stay down in football.

At underage levels I was always part of strong sides that were used to winning. This, of course, did nothing to ease my sense of myself, but it did help to hone the edge of my desire to improve.

A typical week for me would entail a gym session on a Monday, training on a Tuesday, another gym session on a Wednesday, training again on a Thursday, a pre-match briefing session on a Friday, followed by a match on either a Saturday or a Sunday. It might vary a little depending on the time of year or the stage of competition, but at its core, this was a routine that stayed with me from fifteen to twenty-five.

In school I did the barest minimum to get me by. Dad was often absent while Mammy juggled the demands of seven children and the realities of a slowly disintegrating relationship with her husband. As a result, it wasn't reasonable to expect to be ferried to and from my varied sporting commitments. But that was no obstacle. If I needed to cycle to training or pester a lift to training or thumb a ride to training, then that was what I would do and so be it.

Football continued like that pretty much unabated right the way through until minor level, at which stage the realities of inter-county football began to make themselves understood to us.

***

Roscommon is a small county in what is typically considered the poorest and most rural of Ireland's provinces. Mayo and Galway have historically dominated the region, and in turn have frequently found themselves dominated by teams from Munster and Leinster.

If you take a brief look at the history books you will find that Connacht hold less than half the number of All-Ireland Football Championships than either of those other two provinces, only ranking ahead of Ulster in the country. Roscommon have made the final just five times. We've only won it twice, the last of those victories coming way back in 1944. The Sam Maguire trophy is a long-absent visitor to our borders. That's just how things are in this part of the world.

The minor level of inter-county football, which during my time was an Under–18 age group, is where we began to lose. And this continued up into the Under–21s as well.

In our provincial championship we would be well able to stand to the likes of Leitrim and Sligo and Longford, but as sure as grass is green, and as sure as shit stinks in the sun, sooner or later we'd come up against either Mayo or Galway. This was the point at which we'd lose.

Sometimes those losses could be quite heavy.

It didn't matter that we weren't *expected* to win. We wanted to win. We needed to win. I needed to win. So, those losses hurt. My roll of honour at underage inter-county level, such as it is, looks something like this:

In 2004 we lost the Under–16 Connacht final to Galway. In 2007 we lost the Under–21 Connacht final to Mayo, a feat we managed to repeat in 2008. We did manage to win the 2008 Connacht Junior final, beating Leitrim, but that was quickly followed by losing the All-Ireland junior final to Dublin that same year.

As you can see, we were always there or thereabouts. We were strong enough to get ourselves into contention, but we rarely had that little bit extra to get ourselves over the line.

As the quirks of fate would have it, it seemed that I managed to be born just a little bit too early to taste inter-county victory. Because, invariably, my growth out of one footballing age group and into another would almost always seem to coincide with a period of unparalleled success for the team that I had just left.

Roscommon won the All-Ireland Minor title in 2006, a year after I'd grown too old for that squad. They won further Connacht Junior titles in 2008 and 2009, again after I had left that team. And they won four Connacht Under–21 titles between 2010 and 2015. I was promoted from the Under–21 team to the senior panel halfway through 2009.

Such is life.

Regardless, between 2004 and 2009 I made my way through the ranks of underage Roscommon football with my shot at eventually making the senior panel still firmly on track. It was while I was in university in Limerick that my chance finally arrived.

I had been playing in the Sigerson Cup, a football competition involving third-level educational institutions, when, in 2009, a man called Fergal O'Donnell made the leap from underage management at the minor level to become the bainisteoir – or manager – of the Roscommon senior football squad.

Fergal was all about organisation, preparation and rigour. Roscommon were prone to habitual drubbings at the hands of the bigger counties, defeats of sometimes eye-watering size, the kind that can really damage the health of a footballing culture within any given county. His plan was to come in and turn us into a side that would be compact, low-lying and hard to beat. His ethos wasn't to shoot for high scores, it was to minimise the potential for mistakes so scoring chances for the opposition would be reduced to a minimum.

To do that, he needed to infuse his squad with young players who would have the fitness he needed, and who would be pliable enough to learn the message he was imparting. And, coming from a successful stint at the underage levels as he did, having won a Connacht title which he had followed up with a shock All-Ireland triumph, he had an excellent idea of the player profile he thought might make the step up to the senior level to help service the vision he had for Roscommon.

I fitted the profile, and so I was in contention to be a part of that vision.

I was due to play in a match for the University of Limerick (UL) in the Sigerson Cup against University College Dublin (UCD). From my starting position as corner-back, I had been set the task of marking Ciarán Lyng, a sharpshooter who was already a regular figure for the Wexford senior football squad and who was due to line up at corner-forward. Fergal O'Donnell was doing the rounds of all the Roscommon players involved with Sigerson teams, and it just so happened that he came along to see me play in this one.

I had a great game. I played well and subdued Ciarán Lyng as a threat. I must have done enough to impress Fergal, anyway, because later that summer when Roscommon were drawn against Wexford in the All-Ireland qualifiers, I got the call. I had made my first senior panel.

I must have been excited. I must have. This was it. I was about to 'make county'. Everything I had done up until this point had been to get me here. All the hundreds of games, the thousands of training sessions. I had finally gotten the call. I had made it.

It must have been wonderful. I'm sure it was.

It's just, I don't really remember it that much. I remember the game against Wexford, but only sort of. And I can guess that I was happy. But that's about it.

Which must sound a little underwhelming.

All I can say is that I must have been focused. It wasn't about making the panel once. It was about making it permanently. And after that, it was about getting into the match-day squad. And beyond that again, it was about getting starts.

Next, next, next. More, more, more.

The drive to keep progressing does not allow much room for delight. In fact, delight is something to be wary of. If you're too happy you can become too comfortable, and with comfort comes complacency, and after that you can kiss your inter-county spot goodbye.

So, my memory is hazy. But I think I must have been happy.

That year, 2009, I played four or five times for Roscommon at senior level. I got that game against Wexford, which was my rematch against Ciarán Lyng. It was a fixture that we ended up winning after a replay, having drawn the first game. Following that, we exited the All-Ireland Championship in the next round of qualifiers, losing to Meath.

But that was okay, Fergal's plan for the future was already in full swing.

He was a big man for evaluation, and this was something he brought straight into his approach to the senior squad. This took the form of both group meetings and one-to-one sessions whereby we'd be encouraged to understand and articulate ourselves as players through our own eyes, the eyes of our management and even those of our opponents. These sessions, especially the one-to-ones, could be quite intense and get very real for some people, as you were coaxed into understanding or confronting some uncomfortable things about yourself.

During one such session between Fergal and myself he asked me to name three things, three labels that I would see in myself, which would describe me from Fergal's point of view. I stumbled over a few suggestions, I tried 'fit' and 'good player', but I wasn't really sure of what was being required of me.

Eventually Fergal asked if I wanted to know what he thought. I did, of course. What he told me was this. I was consistent. I was punctual. And I turned the ball over a lot, meaning that I frequently lost possession. He had the statistical analysis to back this up. He wasn't wrong. I did lose the ball a lot.

This was a bit of a shock. I knew I wasn't a flair player. I'd always known that. And I knew that there were plenty of areas for me in which to improve. But to have it put to me so starkly was revealing. It made me step back and consider; if this was really how this man viewed me as a player, then it was hardly stellar stuff.

But, Fergal continued. Those three things were only labels. He wasn't saying them to me to make me feel bad. He was doing it to empower me. Because labels can be changed. They can be swapped out for other terms, other attributes. Things you want to be there instead of things you don't. By identifying these labels, we were making them known and knowable. And once they were there, they could be controlled.

Control the controllable. It's pretty much what all sports are based on. Especially team sports, where so much is beyond your influence. Fergal was giving me an avenue to improve, to progress, to help establish myself further. That was exactly the sort of thing I wanted.

I came away from that meeting with a goal to improve my possession of the ball, to make sure that I would no longer be the weak link in the team that lost it. If that meant hand-passing safely instead of trying a riskier kick-pass with a potential for a bigger pay-off, then I would hand-pass the ball out of existence. I didn't care. I was going to change that label.

And it was good. I had something to focus on. Something to control. And I made sure that I did.

Sometime after that, we played a challenge match against

GMIT, which went well. During the subsequent video analysis, they pulled up the ball retention statistics and there I was, standing proud at one hundred per cent. I had not given the ball away; I had not lost possession; not once. Fergal made a point of drawing attention to me for praise on this point. And it felt great. It felt like we were progressing. We were reducing our inefficiencies, minimising our mistakes, and maximising our potential to compete.

And we were set up to compete extremely well for the coming year of 2010.

First, though, it must be said – because I'm sure it's obvious – there were drawbacks to this approach; an approach which has come to dominate the game over the last decade in a way that many people say is slowly killing it.

If you're focused only on minimising mistakes, you slowly eliminate the inclination to attack, which is ultimately what will win you a game. Attack is risky. Risk is bad. Risk must be avoided. So, attack is bad. Attack must be avoided.

That happens as a team, but it happens as a player too.

I had already decided to focus on maximising my strengths. However, working under this ethos, I think I was allowed, or I allowed myself, to drive things much too far. Instead of favouring my strengths but still developing other aspects to my game, I became micro-focused on entirely eliminating from my game anything that might be considered a risk.

At club level for Elphin, as one of the better players, I would generally be played further forward than happened at inter-county level. This allowed me to try things, to attempt kick-passes and through balls, to even get in position to attempt the odd score.

At inter-county level, this became anathema. I was good at organising a defence and I had learned not to lose possession. I was fit. I was strong. And that is what I would do. Nothing else.

During my last year of university, this reluctance to even consider anything that wasn't defensive became very apparent while I was training with the Limerick senior football squad. Donie Buckley was the fitness coach and selector for Limerick at the time. And during my first session with Limerick, he was in charge.

I wasn't sure of my place in that session. Usually, in Roscommon, I would go into things full throttle. That was no bother. I knew where I stood, I knew what was okay and I knew what was expected. But here I was an outsider. They were doing me a favour by letting me train, and I didn't want to be the stupid hunk of a country lad that came barrelling in without a lick of sense, just looking to kick the head off people. So, in absence of knowing better, I decided to hold back.

The training session progressed with me tipping away at roughly half-pace. At some stage, a ball came in that under normal circumstances I would have taken easily, but in an effort to rein myself in, I let my mark take the ball and move possession away. Donie blew on his whistle, bringing things to a halt, and strode out onto the pitch. I was busy complimenting myself on not buckling the Limerick lad, so I didn't notice that Donie was coming for me until he was right on top of me.

Ronan, isn't it? Donie asked.

Yes, I replied.

How you getting on? You okay? You're not injured or anything?

No, no. I'm all good.

You sure?

Totally.

Right then.

Donie took a deep breath in; then he unleashed.

So what the FUCK are you doing letting that man take that ball? All day. All fucking day. That ball should have been yours all fucking day. You should have cleaned him out of it. You should have gone through him.

He took a short pause, only enough for him to get some oxygen in his lungs and for me to wipe the spittle from my eyes, then he continued.

I don't want to see you holding back for nothing in here. If you're going to be at that, you can just fuck off away out of it right now. Fuck off back to Roscommon. Do you hear me? You hit hard or you go home. Do you understand?

I nodded dumbly. Donie took this for assent.

Good, he said, his voice dropping immediately back to a conversational tone. Let's pick up where we stopped.

Donie had given me permission to be myself, and all of a sudden I was off the leash. From there I began to learn in a way that I hadn't done in a while.

In another session under Donie's guidance, we were set to a drill designed to get everyone attempting to score points. This is something I had almost entirely stopped doing, and it definitely had me nervous about making a fool of myself, a fear caused by the garden of one 'Ructions', a taxi driver who operated in the Elphin area. He was known as Ructions because wherever he went, ructions were exactly what usually followed him.

Ruction's garden was beside the local football pitch. It was neither directly behind, nor particularly close to the goalposts, and the ball would have to clear the back net, a large oak tree and the high wall that enclosed the garden by a fair distance to make it that far. Now, I may have had a reputation for landing the odd O'Neills size-five football right into Ruction's garden. It got to such a stage that the phrase 'landing one in Ruction's garden' became a term used for all situations where someone may have missed the mark by more than a little.

It was a humiliating thing to have happen to you. The jeers and sarcastic cheers would rise up from your teammates, forming a bitter chorus which bent your head groundwards in shame as you trotted off the pitch and hopped the stonewall into Ruction's garden to retrieve the ball.

As we lined up to do Donie's point-scoring drill during that session in Limerick, this was all I could think of. More than anything else, I did not want to end up in Ruction's garden. Let me do anything but that.

I took my place and watched the other lads take their shots at goal until it was my turn. I caught the ball that was tossed to me, ran forward a few paces and then put my foot through it, leathering it with the full force of my desire not to make a fool of myself. Then I watched, we all watched, as the ball ballooned away from the posts and way, way, way out into the distance. If this had been in Elphin that ball wouldn't have just made Ruction's garden, it would have cleared it and ended up in the local cattle mart.

My head dropped and I braced for the bollocking or the humiliation that I was sure would be coming my way.

Donie cleared his throat to shout.

Good fucking man, Ronan, he roared. Good stuff. Did you see that, lads? He didn't leave anything behind him with that effort. You can't fault that. You just can't. Great stuff. Great connection, Brady. Well done.

I trotted to the back of the line bemused but thrilled. Here was a scenario in which failure at full tilt was considered a success. It was a wonderful sensation, made all the more alluring by the contrast of what I was becoming used to back in Roscommon, where that sort of profligacy would have been regarded as the ultimate sin.

I found that I loved it. I wasn't built to play it safe. I was built to be a wrecking ball. A one-man demolition crew in the middle of the park, there to break things up and move them forward.

But if I wanted to keep my place in the senior squad, I could not do this. So, I didn't. And while that had short-term benefits, in the long run I think it held my senior career back. I became too safe and too conservative, which ultimately made me too ineffectual to ever be considered a vital part of the team.

That's not to blame Fergal. I have very few regrets about how I conducted myself or how I used my time or my talent during the period of my inter-county career, but there is a part of me that wonders what might have happened if I had cut loose just a little more.

In 2010, under Fergal's guidance, Roscommon won the Connacht title for the first time in nine years. I was part of that squad, but, frustratingly, I was only on the fringes of the team. I was always part of the panel, and I would generally make the match-day twenty-three, which comprised fifteen players and eight substitutes. Occasionally, I would get a run as a substitute, but it was only rarely, if ever, that I got a start.

I can't tell you the specifics of which games I played in or subbed for or missed altogether because I don't know. I do know that I didn't make the pitch the day that we won the Connacht final, and while that was disappointing, I was okay with it because I knew, one hundred per cent, that I had given my all to try and make it and had simply come up short. I could handle that. I had controlled the controllable. As long as I had done that, I could swallow the disappointment of not being picked.

After that was the All-Ireland quarter final in Croke Park against Cork. It was a game that we fancied as a team. We thought that, if things went right, if we did what we knew we could, we would be able to take Cork that day. And what was more is that I was in line to play.

Playing in Croke Park is pretty much the pinnacle of experience and achievement that most inter-county players can hope for. Realistically, of the thirty-three teams that play at senior level (Kilkenny don't play football, but New York and London do), there's only really eight or so that have a realistic chance of ever winning the Sam Maguire. So, getting to Croker is a huge, huge deal. It's the place of legend.

The GAA may have been born in Thurles during the 1880s at the Hayes Hotel with the soon-to-be Semple Stadium only a short distance away, but it is Croke Park that holds the imagination of most fans and players. It's the heartbeat of every daydream and ambition. It's the backdrop to every All-Ireland final you'll ever have seen. You grow up watching people duel from within the sweep of its tiered stands, which form a towering amphitheatre pointing towards the terraced history of Hill 16, the memory of the 1916 Rising and the 1920 Bloody Sunday massacre still entwined deep within the roots of the structure, endowing the whole place with a mythic sense of importance.

It's a special place, and I was potentially going to play there.

Then I got injured, and suddenly this dream seemed like something that would evaporate.

It was my hamstring. Something had happened to make it feel like it was on the verge of snapping. Not stretching. Not straining. Not tearing. Snapping. It was brutal. With every step and stride I took, my leg screamed at me; one inch further, it said, and I could kiss the whole muscle goodbye.

I immediately took myself to the physio, where we did a variety of strength and flexibility tests to assess the situation. We did everything the physio could think of, prodding it, flexing it, stretching it, working it, after which we had a conversation that went something like this.

Well, Ronan, I don't know what to say to you.

How bad is it? I asked, with strains of 'The Final Countdown' rebounding through my head for reasons I didn't fully understand.

It's perfect, he replied.

Perfect?

The muscle is strong. There's no issue. It's not about to snap. It's not about to go. It's absolutely fine.

That can't be right.

Why can't it?

Because I'm in agony.

That may very well be the case, but that's not coming from the muscle.

But every step feels awful.

If it was about to go, you wouldn't have been able to do any of the exercises we've just done. The muscle is absolutely fine. It must be a nerve problem.

Of course, it's a nerve problem! I almost yelled at him. I'm nervous about my hamstring splitting in half and hitting into my ass from the force of the recoil.

I don't know what to tell you, the physio said. I'm as certain as I can be that it's simply a nerve that's gotten itself trapped or something similar. Whatever it is, it's sending you a faulty pain signal. Your hamstring is as fine as it's ever been. You're grand and strong.

But what about the match?

From my perspective, you're good to play. All I can suggest is some painkillers to lessen the sensation coming from the nerve.

None of this news was satisfying. He wasn't saying it was all in my head. He'd no doubt that I was feeling the pain. All he was saying was that it was as good as a phantom pain, because it didn't really *mean* anything. I wasn't about to have my hamstring blast asunder with the bang of a gunshot. I could play if I wanted to.

That's easier said than done. It's hard to trust in science when your body is a true believer in magic. My body had conjured up this pain, and it was bluntly refusing to accept that everything was essentially okay.

Imagine it. Wherever you are right now – reclining, sitting, standing – stretch out your leg and try to imagine a screw-twist of pain shooting up through the back of your thigh as you do it, a simmering feeling that your leg contains an explosive that's on the very cusp of detonating. It wasn't that my leg felt bad when I ran or when I sprinted, it was that my leg felt bad every time I moved.

I could rationally understand what the physio had said to me, and I certainly agreed with the prognosis he had delivered, but, try as I might, I could not bring myself to believe in him. It filled me with a doubt that was impossible to shake.

And I was supposed to play the biggest match of my life,

step out on the sacred turf of Croke Park, the place where my heroes played, and deliver a full-throttle performance in aid of the team – all with this cascade of doubt swirling through my head.

It was a shite situation.

I'm a competitive guy. I felt that we might be able to beat Cork. The rest of the team felt the same way. I wanted to win. They wanted to win. And now I was thinking that, if I couldn't pass myself as fully fit, then I had no right being out on that pitch, because we needed fifteen players out there leaving nothing behind. How could I do that with a leg I felt I could no longer trust? What happened if I got out there and missed something, a tackle or a ball or a pass, because in the back of my head I was carrying this doubt about myself? I didn't want to be the person who put themselves before the team. Not when there was so much at stake.

Fergal wanted to match me up against the Cork sharp-shooter, Ciarán Sheehan. He was a skilful and powerful player, and I was generally pretty good at disrupting those guys. I had watched all the footage: videos of his dummies, his favoured foot, kicking style, how he created space. I felt that I was good enough to do a job on him, I was prepared and ready – in every way except for my fucking hamstring. I told this to Fergal O'Donnell and the rest of the management team, and they said to see how it went.

Before the match we conducted a fitness test on the leg. Again, I was put through my paces: running, sprinting, passing, kicking, turning, twisting. Again, I passed everything with flying colours. Again, my hamstring pulsed with the threat of explosion with each and every move.

Very bluntly, I was given the opportunity to pass myself fit for the match.

And I declined. I didn't feel fit. I wanted to win the match more than I wanted to play in it. And I thought fifteen players who weren't carrying my doubts would give us the best chance of victory.

We played. We lost. Cork would eventually go on to win the All-Ireland that year. I rode the bench and never came on.

I would also never again come so close to playing in Croke Park. The following year I would once again make the bench for an All-Ireland qualifier against Tyrone in Croke Park, but again we would lose and again I wouldn't play. But I wasn't in contention for that match as much as I was for the game against Cork.

Not playing that day against Cork is the biggest regret of my football career.

Looking back now, I do not think any of my reasoning was incorrect. I can understand my thinking and agree with it. But I am convinced that I should have just played anyway.

I should have sucked it up and gone out there to see what happened. I should have popped the painkillers, gritted my teeth against the agony in my hamstring and ridden the waves of doubt through as long of the match as I could have managed.

But I didn't, and that was that.

The key opportunity in my football career had come and gone. But I wouldn't understand that for a few years yet.

***

After missing the game against Cork, I made the decision that 2011 would be my year. I would train harder, I would push further, and I would give myself the best possible opportunity of becoming a regular member of the Roscommon team. No more riding the bench. Not if I could help it.

This was going grand. I was training with every ounce of energy I could muster. I sacrificed everything before the altar of making an indispensable county player out of myself. I was competing for places. I felt like I was getting somewhere.

At that time I was teaching out in Carrickmacross in Monaghan. One of the evenings out there some friends convinced me to take part in a game of five-a-side soccer on an all-weather pitch.

This was the sort of thing that us inter-county players were absolutely not supposed to do. But I enjoyed soccer. I always had. I'd played it to a decent level. I'd even had the opportunity of joining Longford town, a club with the League of Ireland that would have given me a shot at making a semi-professional sporting life for myself. That was during my teenage years and I was pretty good. At the age of sixteen I even managed to win the Under–21 award for player of the year, so I definitely would have had a shot at it if I'd wanted to give it a go. But eventually I'd chosen football instead. I still enjoyed having a kick around, and I genuinely didn't think there would be any harm to it.

More fool me.

I played the match and went over on my ankle very badly. It was hard to walk on and this was a disaster for a few reasons. I couldn't tell them that I'd been playing soccer, because that might be the end of me right then and there, but I was also in line to play a challenge match for Roscommon in a few days. This was supposed to be my year, and I was in line to start for a change. This was the type of opportunity that I couldn't let go of again.

That night I iced the ankle and hoped for the best. The next day it was a stiff and puffy tangle of pain. I couldn't believe that I'd been as stupid as to do this to myself. Not now.

I couldn't make it into school, I couldn't walk on it. At lunchtime some of the staff dropped down crutches to me at home so I could get myself out of the house and come up to the school to teach for the second half of the day. Once the school day had finished, I called the team management and told them that there was no point in me making the four-hour round trip to training as I could barely walk. They disagreed. They wanted me there, even if it was only so the team physio could give my ankle a look.

I packed myself into the car and set off for Roscommon. Over the course of the two-hour drive, using the ankle to work the pedals, I must have loosened it out some, because by the time I landed down it wasn't feeling as bad as it had before.

I took myself over to the physio and made up some nonsense story about turning my ankle while at work. I'd have preferred to amputate the ankle than to tell him the truth. He tested it for flexibility and strength and once again gave me the opportunity to pass myself fit. I could play and stay in the twenty-three players that comprised the match-day squad or I could rest up and fall out of that group. This was supposed to be my year. If I dropped out of the twenty-three now, there was a distinct chance I wouldn't get back in again, and that would be the whole thing fucked.

No way. Not this time.

I said I'd be grand and asked him to strap the ankle up as tightly as he could. This left me with just about enough mobility to run, sprint and kick. I played the game and did pretty well, but I would never play without my ankle strapped ever again.

I would play the rest of the year with the injury, icing my ankle after every match or training session to reduce the swelling, never at one hundred per cent, always trying to break myself in order to push my way into the team, and never quite managing to pull it off.

My 2011 season was pretty much summed up in a Connacht Championship game against New York in New York. I went out hoping to make the starting team, never mind the bench. But when the squad was called out, I hadn't even made the twenty-three. I was back-up to the back-up. This was supposed to be my year, but I wasn't even making the bench.

Oh well. Next year will be my year, I said to myself.

I got to a stage where I was continually asking myself the question: Will this help my game? Which is ridiculously reductive, but it's how I approached everything: holidays, weddings, life events of practically any nature, you just didn't plan for them because you simply assumed that you'd miss them. They weren't going to benefit your game, so they weren't things that were going to happen for you.

It was micro-focus. I was always working towards the next short-term something; the next ball, the next game, the next training session, the next, the next, the next – always thinking about football. How can I improve? What am I doing to improve? Why isn't everyone else around me trying to do this the way I am?

Next, next, next. More, more, more.

Back at my club in Elphin we were very competitive at the time. We were competing for county titles. In 2010 and 2011 we made it to back-to-back county finals for the first time since the 1950s. It was a big deal. Unfortunately, on both occasions we came up short to St Brigid's of Kiltoom, but St Brigid's went on to the All-Ireland club final, losing to the great Crossmaglen Rangers by a goal. That gave us hope. Maybe we weren't that far off?

It's the tiniest of margins that end up deciding the outcome of a whole season. It's less than inches in the difference between winning and losing. And that became my mentality. We needed to find those inches, find them and close them to bridge that tiny gap between success and failure. It all counted: missed gym sessions, lads out socialising, or niggling injuries that meant they didn't train. I was looking around at them and thinking, do they even want this?

I became frustrated with the rest of my teammates. They inevitably had other things going on in their life, some good, some bad; some of them would likely have been struggling with some genuinely serious issues while I was sat beside them, openly resenting the fact that they weren't giving as much to this cause as I was. If I was doing it, then it didn't matter what was going on with them, they should be doing it too. It made me arrogant, which wasn't fair to anyone around me.

This doesn't make for a well-rounded individual. I can only imagine what I was like to my family and friends. And I'm not sure it makes for a helpful teammate either.

Culturally, we lionise stories of sportspeople who have a single-minded drive to succeed, a one-track obsession that completely devours everything else. But is that any way to live? How happy are those people? What difference do all the medals in the world make if you had to become a miserable prick at heart just to attain them?

The problem is that, while you're in that way of thinking, you don't have the capacity to see outside of it. There's no space to step back and regard things from a slightly more removed and healthy point of view. That was true for me. I didn't have the space or the maturity to understand that perhaps, just perhaps, this micro-focus was actually detracting from my footballing ability, that I was leading myself to a place of diminishing returns and, maybe, burnout.

It wasn't until I stopped being obsessed with every little gain in every single session that I was able to take a breath and go, wait a second, this is all a bit mad, isn't it? What am I doing?

Let's look at what I've got here; I've got a life totally devoted to these goals ... of what? Winning another provincial championship? Doing well enough in the All-Ireland, making a quarter or semi-final? Because, being wholly realistic, there was only ever a very minute chance we'd win the thing.

Then it comes down to how you define success. What does success look like individually and as a collective? Because if success is winning the All-Ireland, then, and I hate to say it, every single ounce of effort is going to be wasted in failure, because more than likely, that just ain't going to happen, no matter how hard you bust your back to try and make it so. It means that ninety-nine per cent of people involved in the sport are also failures, which is just a horrible way to conceive of things.

That means you either need to define success in some other way – which could be absolutely anything, like working as part of a team, being competitive in any match you play, moving from club to county or from panel to squad or from bench to starting line-up – or, and this was the big one, by having fun.

Fun was something that football had ceased to be for me. By being so focused on what was next, what I had to improve, where we were going, I wasn't coming out of matches thinking that I'd enjoyed them. I might have accomplished something, but I don't think I'd really enjoyed it.

What brought me to this point was, and no prizes for guessing, an injury caused by over-training. I got an inflammation injury in my pelvis called osteitis pubis, which essentially means that in the pubic symphysis, where the two main pubic bones meet, a bit of space occurs within the cartilage, allowing the bones to move in a way they shouldn't, which causes the whole thing to swell up.

It was a funny sort of injury because it didn't exactly stop me from playing, but it did mean that it would take me days to recover. It got so bad that I found myself having to roll over onto my tummy to get myself out of bed because I couldn't sit up and swing myself out as you usually would.

I tried to play through it for a while. I put my head down, gritted my teeth and played the games as best I could. And that was okay for a while, but the pain slowly built up and up, getting worse and worse until I found myself in the position of having to make a choice. My first option was to take some injections directly into my pelvis to ease the inflammation or simply mask the pain, which would be grand, but wouldn't solve the issue entirely: it would only make it bearable. The other option was to take some time out and let it heal on its own. And from where I was, both mentally and physically, that was a much more appealing option.

That's what I did. I could barely believe it myself, as it seemed to fly in the face of the way I had sought to position my life beforehand. But I'm not too sure that I intellectualised the decision overmuch. I think that, at the time, I would have been much more step-orientated about it. I was injured. Time off would help the injury. That would improve my football. I think that's how I took it. But of course, I was burnt out. I'd flogged myself half to death with my fierce commitment to my micro-focused mentality, and just because I wasn't able to articulate it in those terms doesn't mean that this wasn't what was really underpinning my decision.

We're all driven by internal workings all the time. All that changes is how much we acknowledge and recognise that.

All of a sudden I found myself with space to do things of my choosing. Previously I had *chosen* to impose an intense footballing life on myself, but it hadn't really felt like that at the time. It had felt like I was almost obligated to do it. And now that I was out, even if only temporarily, I felt that I wasn't tied to this never-ending cycle of training and club and training and county and training.

I had room to breathe, to step back and assess my life as I had been living it. It didn't happen all at once. It couldn't; I was too wound up for that. I needed time. You can't just stop something and expect your body to understand. It needs to unspool itself and slow down.

So, as the weeks spun out into months, and as my body and mind finally unclenched, I was able to find some space to have a look at the decisions I'd made, the routines I'd been in, the mentality I had adopted. I was able to lay it all out before me and see it from a remove. And once I was there, I couldn't help but wonder: what had I been doing it all for?

I didn't have a good answer. With just a few months' distance, it had already taken on an air of madness to me – these things I had been doing, these hardships I had been inflicting upon myself. They no longer seemed reasonable or warranted. They appeared weird. It opened me up to the idea that maybe I could do other things as well. It put me in a place where I was willing to explore other experiences.

Like circus.

SEVEN

TOURING YOURSELF

(Aliens, sleepy time and the challenges of being
socially conservative.)

I was an alien with extraordinary abilities.

Well, sort of.

I was actually a *support* to an alien with extraordinary abilities. This was according to the US department of immigration at least.

Panti Bliss was the alien to whom I provided support. In fact, the entire *Riot* cast and crew were officially designated as supports to Panti for the purposes of our performing visas when visiting the States.

Let none of ye forget it, Panti would proclaim. I am the talent.

And she was.

With her and the rest of the troupe, I toured the world with *Riot* for three years. From 2016 to 2019 we took in places like Sydney, Melbourne, New York and Toronto. We returned to Dublin almost once a year to play sold-out runs in Vicar Street. It was a thrilling ride that helped me learn exactly what would be involved if I were to become a full-time, lifelong artist: the dedication required, the sacrifices demanded, the highs and lows of it, all the glittering possibility and equally likely destitution.

It also challenged my attitude towards sexuality further than it had ever been challenged before. I mistakenly thought that, in swallowing the mores of my country-bred youth to be a part of the show in the first place, I had overcome the worst of my learned biases regarding the fluidity of sexual preferences. I was now a stripper in a show about queer culture, for goodness sake. Assless chaps were no longer an unknown quantity to me. Surely I had progressed?

In some ways, I had. In others, not so much.

This first became apparent directly following our Dublin premiere. I can be an active presence on social media, and in the wake of the show the direct messages I received on platforms like Instagram took a sharp turn towards the sexual.

I wouldn't say that I was inundated. This wasn't the burlap sacks full of fan mail that you would imagine someone like Marilyn Monroe or Elvis Presley to have received. But it was significant. My inbox began to fill quite regularly. After each performance, it didn't take long for the little light on my phone to illuminate as people swiftly succeeded in digitally tracking me down.

Most of the messages were from men. And most of them were perfectly fine. But some of them … well, I would call them *suggestive,* but only in the same way that hardcore porn is *suggestive* of sex. They were quite forward.

I wasn't used to that, but, you know, I'm a cool guy. I could be cool with this sort of thing.

Couldn't I?

Then there was the fact that being part of a queer show about queer culture with plenty of queer people involved meant that, inevitably enough, we regularly ended up in a lot of queer places for our after-show drinks.

As a fine and upstanding young Roscommon lad, I was used to pubs and clubs as God had intended them: sticky underfoot from spilled bottles of Smirnoff Ice and with the smell of Guinness-orientated flatulence pervading all of the furnishings. On the odd occasions when I found myself on the beer in Dublin, I would usually gravitate towards places like Kehoe's, or Flannery's or Coppers because, well, that was the normal thing to do.

Those were not the types of places I found myself in with *Riot*. These places were higher-end establishments where the polite thing to do was to keep the power of your flatulence firmly stored inside the fabric of your trousers.

We're talking mosaic-tiled floors, patent red leather and shining stainless steel, not sawdust and vomit. We're talking gimlets, coupes and highballs, not pint glasses and plastic shot cups. And most of all, we're talking a deeply varied mix of people from different cultures, creeds and sexualities, not the lads from the town throwing some shapes down the back with white trainers and a Superdry jacket.

This was how I suddenly found myself in large groups of people, many of whom I now considered friends, where, for the first time in my life, the straight people were thoroughly outnumbered by the gay people.

From where I am right now, here and today, this is not strange at all. I've had some of the best times of my life in those scenarios. Nowadays, I'd be far more likely to end up in Sam's Bar than I would in Coppers. But, back then, it was super-weird.

Back home when I was growing up we didn't really have 'the gays'. I mean, we did, of course, but we didn't too. People who were gay either kept it to themselves or moved away. Those were the only two realistic options for the non-straight folks of Roscommon and similar rural Irish settings.

Everyone at home was straight. If you wanted to be part of the pack, you were straight. If you weren't, then you weren't part of the pack. This was regrettable and shameful, but it was how things were. I wanted to be part of the pack, and you're sure-as-shit that I was straight. Straightest guy in the *room*, so I was. Straightest guy *ever*! If you say otherwise, then I'll fight you and I'll show you. By God, I'll show you!

Sad, but true.

Fast forward to *Riot*, and I'm now presenting myself as a stripper, putting myself out there for the entertainment of all genders and all sexualities. (There was a section in my act in *Riot* where I would trick an audience member into kissing me on the lips. Due to rigging and staging, this kiss had to happen at the same chair each night. So be it male, female or anyone in between, I was kissing that person.) I spent my performances gyrating, preening, alluring and vamping as much as I could manage, showering myself in cheese and onion crisps as I seductively removed my Roscommon GAA uniform one sock at a time, all to encourage the attention of the audience and, hopefully, elicit their amusement.

After shows, in the venue or subsequently in the bar, it would be quite natural for audience members and friends of the cast or crew to approach and have the chats. For many, that's all it ever was. For others, there was an edge of flirtation around it, which was perfectly fine too.

A lot of the time it was women, which was the kind of attention I was used to and very comfortable in receiving. I never had any intention of taking it beyond that. I love Michelle and I'm comfortable in my monogamy, but who doesn't like the flattery of flirtatious attention? I certainly do and, when it came from women, I would lap it up like a purring cat.

But of course, if wasn't just women who approached me. Very often it was men, which was something I had no experience with, and I had to work hard to become comfortable with this.

It was initially very uncomfortable, not only because I didn't know how to politely disentangle myself from the situation, but also because I was still very concerned about not coming across as gay.

Why?

Well, deep within me, the notion that I might be thought of as gay was still copper-fastened to this idea of social exclusion, of not being part of the main pack, of moving away.

For instance, where I came from, the term 'gay' was a catch-all for anything negative. Let's say I was to turn up at the disco in a pink T-shirt. That would be gay. Obviously. Someone would call me gay, and I would continue to be called gay until I removed it. If I didn't remove it, I would actually become gay in the eyes of the group, which was a bad thing and could lead to the aforementioned exclusion from the pack.

But it was also a negative in an absolute sense. If something was bad or crap or disappointing, then it was gay.

Lose a match after an unjust sending-off? That's gay.

Reach for a bowl of cereal and discover that there's no milk? That's gay.

Be asked to take out the bins only to have the bag split on you and ruin your shoes? That's definitely gay.

None of that has anything to do with actually being gay, aside from the fact that they're all negatives, and being homosexual was considered the cardinal negative, the biggest of all the unforgivables. And we would reinforce gayness as a negative by saying it again and again and again.

It's strange to say, but it was almost unintentional. We absorbed this way of thinking and acting and talking from the world around us, so this all felt natural, like this was exactly how we were supposed to feel. Of course, gayness was a negative. It felt that way. It just was.

That's how language works. It reinforces and confines just as easily as it can liberate and explore. Our language and our outlook was to label anything remotely homosexual as something to be exposed and avoided.

It makes change hard. Because change feels like an attack

on who you are and how you are 'wired'. The instinct is to dig your heels in and resist. I don't need to change – this is what you try to convince yourself of. I'm grand, you say. It's everything and everyone else that needs to adjust. I'm the normal one. I'm the one who is in the right.

But you're not. And that can be the hardest thing in the world to accept.

I wasn't stupid. I knew that I had taken a headlong dive into queer culture; that, to a certain extent, I would have to expand my boundaries. I would be put in situations that I found uncomfortable and that I would have to, rightly, learn to normalise.

But there is a stark difference between understanding something and feeling something. And for the first few tours of *Riot*, I felt like I was constantly in danger of being mistaken for gay, and it terrified me. I could understand that it shouldn't. But learning to feel that way was a much harder thing to achieve.

By the time I'd brought myself into *Riot*, I had thought I was okay with most things homosexual. I was cool with it, wasn't I?

I thought I was.

But I soon discovered that by the time I'd gotten over my reluctance to engage with the contents of the show, by the time I found myself at the heart of this vibrant and successful, celebratory piece of queer culture, I still had within me this deep-seated, insidious idea that being LGBTQ+ was all very well and good, more power to you, but only as long as you did it somewhere else. You can be gay, but don't be gay in here in front of me. Have a bit of decency and keep it private. Keep it elsewhere. And definitely, definitely, definitely don't try and draw me into it.

It's not my proudest moment, but it is the truth, and it took me a long while to figure out that I was, in fact, very, very far from being okay with things.

And there was this other thing. For some reason, it was easier for me to accept a female who was lesbian than it was to accept a man who was gay. I can only imagine that I must have perceived the former as a curio and congratulated myself on my successful display of cosmopolitanism for accepting lesbians as part of the group, while the latter was a threat that I felt sprang at me from an almost conscious level. The lesbians were safe, from my point of view – they'd never want anything physical from me – but the gay men, I couldn't be so sure about them.

All of this made navigating the after-show world of *Riot* and the male-to-male flirtations I encountered all the more treacherous, because I was left constantly unsure about what was a quasi-homophobic reluctance on my part, and what was actually inappropriate behaviour from these other men.

The boundaries between one and the other were blurred for me because I wasn't confident or comfortable in myself. I knew rationally that it was both hypocritical and unfair of me to bask in the attention from women then recoil at the attention from men. Besides, now that I had an increasing array of gay friends, how could I in good conscience maintain an attitude that bordered on disgust whenever another guy made a pass at me?

It was an ugly part of my character, so I determined to open myself out.

Men would approach and they would flirt, and I would do my best to be cool. I would joke and laugh and play along while inwardly I tried to talk myself out of being as taut as a bowstring ready to snap.

And, over time, it worked. The more I exposed myself to it, the more I understood that my world would not fall in around me should I accept and enjoy a compliment from another man. It was as natural as a female compliment and, I soon discovered, it was pleasant.

Most of the time, anyway.

Placing yourself in a sexual context, even one designed specifically for laughs rather than thrills, can have the effect of turning you into a sexual object devoid of other characteristics in the eyes of a few. It was like that because I had presented myself to them in a certain way: since I had put myself in front of them as a stripper in a show, they felt entitled to treat me differently, like I was fair game.

Most of the time, with most of the men I encountered, it was fine; a normal-enough flirty sort of situation that you can politely rebuff with no harm intended or felt. Some of the time, however, it could be very forward, getting quite handsy and physical.

Aggressive sexuality is possession-based. It's domination and ownership. They take your personal space and then lay hands on your body so they can try and claim you for their own.

It could be a hand on your arm, or your hip, that slides down to your ass. Or it could be being taken by the waist and hauled away from your group of friends, away from your support, over to meet a new group of people whereby you'd be introduced as 'his'.

It wasn't that they were being threatening or aggressive in a confrontational sense, it was that they were trying to take control, and they were doing it in a way that I hadn't consented to or indicated would be okay.

The first tool I learned to rebuffing this was language.

Again. Language. That tricky devil.

The language I formed around this was almost embarrassingly stark for what I was used to.

Excuse me, can you take your hands off me please.

Or.

I'm really not comfortable with what you're doing. Can you stop that, please?

Or.

I'm not so eager to meet your friends now because of the way you've approached me.

It all sounded so juvenile to my ears. It was cringeworthy stuff. Being this abrupt not only felt rude, it felt violent, like I was the one who was radically out of line, which did nothing to assuage the doubts I had about my own attitudes towards homosexuality. Because, even in that, those phrases that I learned to deliver seemed almost too polite compared to what

I was actually feeling. What my inner voice really wanted me to say was, in no uncertain terms, get your fucking hands off me.

And I couldn't say that. I didn't trust myself. I didn't trust my intentions.

By and large, these phrases would work. The other guy would step back and apologise and that would be that, boundary laid, and limits respected. But occasionally it wouldn't.

I would say my piece and the offending person would step back, throw up a hand, utter an apology, all smiles and consolations. But very quickly the hand would be back, on my arm or my hip or my ass, and the cycle would repeat. Worse than a fly hovering around dogshit, it would just buzz and buzz and buzz until it got its fill.

What, I asked myself, was I supposed to do then? My social upbringing had led me to believe that this sort of invasive and persistent behaviour from a man was nothing short of outright provocation, which should and probably would lead us towards a physical altercation.

That's what I had to learn to deal with, both internally and externally. I was forced into a position of confrontation with myself. I was now not only having to address the biases that I had internalised from my upbringing regarding homosexuality, I was also in a place whereby I was experiencing the same kind of physical intimidation to which women are subjected every day in almost every aspect of life, and it was eye-opening.

I'm not particularly tall or particularly bulky, but I am

strong. I can hold my own. If things get physical I will be able to give an account of myself, even in those situations where I might be overmatched. But the same is not true for many women who find themselves cornered by someone who is making them feel physically uncomfortable. They are in a position whereby, if things go bad – and I mean the not-rare-enough occasions where it goes criminally bad – there might not be anything they can do about it. That must be bone-chillingly scary, but it is the fear that so many women are burdened with.

And, as if things weren't bloody difficult enough from a female's point of view, there's also the bitch factor.

When I say, 'Please stop that', I'm running the risk of being rude or confrontational. When a woman says it, she's running the risk of being labelled 'a bitch', which is a tag designed to attach itself to someone and follow them around.

A bitch is a social pariah. Bitchiness is vicious and unreasonable. It is a term built to cast assertiveness in women as a negative, as something to be avoided and exposed.

Again, it comes down to language reinforcing a male and straight status quo. Gay as a negative. Female assertiveness as bitchiness.

One peculiar thing about these post-show interactions (of which the vast majority were entirely excellent in nature and experience, so please don't misinterpret this as me portraying the after-show world as a gauntlet of sexual harassment: it wasn't and isn't) was that the possessive, handsy behaviour was not confined solely to men.

Once again, because I presented myself in the show as a hyper-sexualised, striptease character, some women would confuse the performed character with my actual self, assuming or presuming that one bled into the other, and so it was okay to treat me differently from how they might treat someone else.

This would generally manifest itself as a freedom to lift up my shirt and rub my abs or squeeze my bicep or, same as the dudes, grab my ass. It would often happen in social circles: a group of us would be standing in a pub or a club whereby the woman in question may have been a friend of cast and crew and would do this in front of everyone.

Liking flirtatious attention does not mean that I am overly fond of being groped by a person of any gender, and I'm not sure my partner Michelle would be too chill about it either.

But I often felt caught by it. Frozen. It would leave me flummoxed as to what to do. Because in not saying anything I felt hypocritical against what I would have done should it have been a man in place of a woman.

I also felt conflicted because if the situation were to be reversed, and I were to stroke her stomach, then it would be a huge deal, and rightly so.

Most importantly, perhaps, was the reaction, or lack thereof, from everyone else. There I'd be, surrounded by people I knew, liked and trusted, and none of them would say anything while whomever it may be would lift my shirt and stroke my abs. I would be like, 'Are ye not seeing this?' And of course, they hadn't.

You begin to understand the nature of inappropriate behaviour, how insidious it is, how it belittles and diminishes people, how it invades attitudes almost by stealth, masquerading beneath the cover of dismissal.

Ah, it's only a compliment. Ah, it's only a joke. Ah, it's only a bit of banter.

And yes, it is banter. And yes, it is a joke. But that doesn't mean that it's not inappropriate or that it's cool.

It's true that the content of the show *Riot* was important in helping me challenge the more problematic things about myself, but in many ways it was the culture that surrounded the production, the attitudes of the people involved, the things they did and the lives they led that did more to aid my self-development than anything else.

And, aside from the lessons in sexual conduct, what I got was a revealing insight into these artists at the top of their game.

These were professionals who were confident in their talent and well aware of what it took to keep themselves in shape, physically and mentally. They became role models to me in what I could possibly do myself.

The people who sang on the show would always be careful of their voices before and after performances. If this meant not really talking, then they didn't talk. If it required them to skip some of the social occasions attached to the tour, the after-show drinks and what have you, then they would skip them, no issues and no problems. The job came first.

It sounds stupid now, but I still don't think that at that

stage I appreciated performance as *proper* work. It wasn't *really* a job. It was a bit of craic, a lark.

This was totally wrong. True, artists can play hard, but they work as hard and oftentimes an awful lot harder than other people with *normal* careers. And while I'd paid lip service towards the idea of committing myself to this path, I still hadn't fully accepted it.

I was well over a year into my career break from teaching. I'd had to let go of my secure work position from my previous school when they'd refused to extend my leave of absence into a second year, which meant that if I was to go back to that profession I would have to interview for new jobs. I was also trying to set myself up with alternative strands of income to fill the gaps between my paid performing gigs, doing personal-training sessions with clients. I thought this might be a flexible job that would allow me to mix the fitness and skill training I had to do anyway with a means of making money. I'd done all of these things, but in many ways I still felt it was all temporary, that at some stage I would go back and return to the way things had been before.

The cast of *Riot* were all lifers. This wasn't a diversion for them, this was a vocation. They lived as artists and they would die as artists too. Rory O'Neill would arrive to a show three hours before I ever got there because that's how long it would take to transform into Panti Bliss. Then Panti would guide the show, never once not performing at full tilt, and she would do that again and again, unquestioningly returning to the well in service of the show and her art.

This wasn't confined to the artists, of course, as the crew were just the same, working long hours to keep the show moving and running and seamless in the eyes of our audiences. It is only by the commitment and skill of a huge array of people that performances can ever achieve the illusion of effortlessness.

I also came to understand that the process of creation never stops. I had thought that you made a show and then you toured the show and that was that. I didn't think you would keep creating the show as you went. But that's exactly what happened with *Riot*. Every time a new tour would roll around, we'd go back into rehearsals and JennyPhilly would recommence the work of honing and tweaking and reassessing and improving the show.

When I watch the videos from those first shows in 2016, with what I thought then was a finished and fine-tuned production, I now realise it was a half-formed thing compared to the show that finished up in Vicar Street in 2019. We never stopped augmenting and discovering, and the show continued to gain strength because of it.

In art as in life, I suppose. We never reach a position whereby we are complete. Whether nine or ninety, we are always works in progress.

Touring with *Riot* exposed in me this disconnect between what I said I was doing and what I felt I was doing. In practice, I had outwardly committed to this performing life, but this commitment was not reflected internally, because doubts continued to gnaw at me: the fear that I was only wasting my own time and Michelle's too, the dread that I'd never be able to make it work financially, the suspicion that this was all just nonsense and I'd be better off going back to teaching.

I was still discovering the capacity we have as people to reveal ourselves to ourselves, and it was increasingly exhausting.

EIGHT

FOOTBALL:
BEGINNING TO END

(The space for circus, Donegal getaways and riding the bench.)

It was a teacher called Shane Holohan who first introduced me to the world of circus. He had been vice-principal in Elphin Secondary School at the time of my year out from football. It was his background in gymnastics and theatre that had led him to the aerial circus art form in the first place. Part of his role in Elphin Secondary School was to oversee the cultural areas of student education. In that vein, he'd started collaborating with Fidget Feet for a school's performance project aimed at working with students to create shows that would then be staged at the Backstage Theatre in Longford.

Inspired by that and eager to learn more, Shane decided to set up circus classes in Carrick-on-Shannon, working out of a gymnastics club in a converted warehouse unit out on the edge of town.

The edge is where you'll always find the circus people. They hang out on the fringe: of towns, cities, communities and cultures. And while initially that was what made their world appear so foreign and foreboding to me, it was similarly what gave it its allure.

It is also what grants these people their vantage point on the world around them. It's what allows them to take what we accept as normal and present it back to us, made strange and fantastic once it has been imbued with their wonderfully askew perspective.

You have to want to find these spaces. But they are always there for you, once you care to look.

It wasn't specifically a conscious decision on my part to go seeking the social and cultural fringe after years of operating firmly in the centre of the most conventional Irish existence possible, but I do believe there was a subconscious pull towards it. Or, more correctly, perhaps it only appeared to be subconscious because, again, it all comes back to an ability to articulate. Without articulation, half-formed thoughts and desires are able to masquerade as instinct. Only now am I able to recognise the patterns of thinking that drove me from one mode of living to another.

That I found circus is the important thing. I began taking Shane's classes in Carrick-on-Shannon as a means of keeping up my fitness by learning to use my body differently while still allowing it time to heal. These classes were based on a mixture of conditioning, flexibility and learning the basics of aerial circus on the standard apparatuses of silks and rope.

I was drawn to it because it was unusual and, importantly, because it was fun, which was something that had leaked out of my footballing life a long time before.

Circus was a slow burn. It wasn't that I got up into the air and found my life immediately changed, although I do know people for whom that is exactly what happened. For me, the circus classes were just interesting and fun enough to keep bringing me back, week after week, allowing what had originally been intended as a brief, diversionary oddity to develop into an actual hobby.

As a person, I've always been a fun-hound, a person eager to have a laugh or a bit of craic, which, when coupled with my tendency to totally immerse myself in things, means that I can quickly form what from the outside might look like an obsessive relationship with my interests. I like things that challenge my limits, physically and mentally, but I also seek out things that have enough room in them to let me develop. I want to be able to get good at something, and all the better if there's no chance of me ever totally mastering it, because all that means is that there will always be new things to find, new experiences to have and new limits to push. This is what happened with skydiving, surfing and football – and now circus.

As the year out of football progressed, my body kept its side of the bargain and healed. It would never be like it had been, of course. In sport you're always losing something: a little bit of strength, a little bit of flexibility, a little bit of power, a little bit of pace. The best athletes are not the ones who try to mask these losses, but the ones who adapt to their circumstances and figure out new ways of remaining competitive in spite of them. They are the ones who understand that ultimately sport is a one-way transaction.

So, I was feeling better, but I would never be the same.

Regardless, I liked the sensation of not always battling myself, not having to tape and strap and coax my body back into battle every day and every week. I was also appreciating the ability to enjoy my life: I had taken a few holidays with Michelle; I had allowed myself some time for the life events that I'd never even considered attending while I was playing football. And, through circus, I was enjoying the challenge of using my body in ways that I was unfamiliar with.

As my interest grew, Shane introduced me to Fidget Feet's Irish Aerial Dance Fest, the annual two-week training camp they hold up in Donegal for beginners, hobbyists and professionals alike.

The IADF happened every summer, and while as a teacher I would always have those months off, I had not had a period without a full schedule of football commitments since I was eight years old, so I'd never truly had a free summer, or a free anything, to indulge myself in something strange and new like this aerial circus boot camp the IADF promised.

The idea of disappearing up into the wilds of the Forgotten County with no one to answer to but myself or Michelle for two weeks was a liberating prospect.

I went up as a lark; two weeks amongst the crusty hippies and bored women in Letterkenny doing God knew what. It might have been a disaster, but I knew I could go in relative anonymity. No one back home would ever need to know.

Once up there, then maybe I would see what this circus thing was about. Perhaps, I suggested to myself, once I saw all the free love and heard all the pretentious artsy waffle that I figured would be the only form of conversation there, then I could safely put paid to the idea of this circus nonsense as a serious hobby.

It would be nice, in a way. It would remove any complications from the return to football and my proper life, which was still very much my intention.

***

I arrived up in Donegal late on a balmy Sunday evening, made sweet and humid by that strange alchemy of climate that schedules our best weather to coincide with the state-wide leaving-cert examinations of our final-year secondary students. I landed into a complex of rickety student apartments that served as the accommodation hub, and over the first few days I slowly got to grips with the running of the festival.

It was spread out over three venues, encompassing the theatre, the community centre and the grand hall of the local leisure centre, which acted as the setting for the vast bulk of workshops and classes on offer.

It's a strange sensation walking into that place. You make your way through the main lobby, past the swimmers, families and regular gym workers, towards the back of the building where the main hall resides. You stroll down a shadowed hallway and press yourself through a set of swing doors, still safely in your normal world. Then, suddenly, you find yourself immersed in an aerial circus wonderland of people hanging from every conceivable fitting and fixture. There are teams of people running across the walls, scores of others contorting themselves into interesting positions on silks and ropes and trapezes, and a low hum of excitement and concentration thrumming from every single person inside. There's a magic in there that's hard to describe, and it's a magic that becomes difficult to resist once you have experienced it.

For two weeks I came under the spell the IADF casts. While, in some ways, I found exactly who and what I had expected up there, I also found so many other things that were entirely beyond what I had imagined.

Not least my own reaction.

Yes, the collection of eighty to ninety people who attended the festival were indeed the mixture of hippies and circus-heads I had envisaged. However, my error had been in thinking that these wouldn't be *my sort of people*. They were. They were mischievous, talented, interesting and, above all, good craic.

The thing about the IADF is that, over the course of its two weeks, it creates a family-style community of people that come to genuinely feel for each other and like each other. You live within the same spaces, you train at the same places, you go out to the same pubs – well, that is, on the odd occasions when you aren't already asleep from pure exhaustion before the evening watershed has come down.

You can get this same thing during any intensive experience. I've had it before with certain teams, or on holidays with groups of people. By going through the same thing with the same people over a focused period of time, you create a bond with them founded on your shared experience. If the time frame is short, it can actually have the effect of strengthening that bond by (mostly) eradicating the time for people to get angry or annoyed with one another, as they would do over the normal course of living in close proximity.

I wasn't expecting that in Donegal, but I got it, nonetheless.

The classes themselves were exhilaratingly hard. They pushed my body beyond what I had thought it capable of. Football strength and football fitness did not really translate to circus strength or circus fitness. I did (and still do) find myself trying to just bull through some of the challenges the classes presented me with, trying to subjugate a given aerial move through a mixture of sheer power and force of will. I quickly discovered that while this approach made certain things possible, it had limited efficiency across an entire routine – as I would spend so much energy trying to do things the wrong way, I would have nothing left to progress from one manoeuvre into the next, which left me totally exhausted and half-crippled, stuck five metres above the ground with a thick cord of rope tangled around my limbs.

If I wanted to get better, I had to learn these things properly – or properly-ish (after all, it's very difficult to totally lead the bull out of the china shop). I had to discipline myself to adopt a new method of thinking about strength, and a different way of training my body.

Each day would leave me stiff, bruised and broken, which should have been exactly what I wasn't looking for in my year away from football, but it did so in such new and interesting ways that I just couldn't help but become enthralled by it.

Circus is not a pain-free existence. I don't want to paint a picture of it as some light-hearted and delicate area of expression. It is not yoga (though maybe I am not doing that right either). It is possibly the toughest thing I have ever put myself through. The people who do this either as a hobby or for a living are people who inflict the most horrific burns, bruises, strains, stretches, extensions and batterings upon themselves. If you didn't know better, you'd deem it sadomasochistic. Why it isn't, or why it isn't for most of us, is because it's not the pain we're in it for – it's the possibility. The possibility of finding out what we are capable of, what we can do with our bodies, and ultimately, how that can lead us into new ways of expressing ourselves.

Because the concept of individual expression was the other thing that I was completely unprepared for. Before, I would have been profoundly uncomfortable with the thought of consciously putting myself out there. It went against the grain.

That's the very Irish idea that prevails when it comes to our view of people in the spotlight. Generally speaking, we don't like it. Occasionally, we can tolerate it, and sometimes we can even revere it, but only up to a point. We want those in the spotlight – be that local, rural or national – to show enough sense, humility and shame for even being there in the first place; we want them to promise to be rightfully uncomfortable about it.

We, as a nation, are hair-trigger sensitive to when we feel someone has gotten too big for their boots. It's a trait in ourselves that I hate, but I'm just as guilty of it as anyone else. If we get even a sniff of someone 'thinking too much of themselves' or getting high on their own sense of self-importance, then we turn on them quite viciously, albeit in our internalised, Irish kind of way. We demote them onto a social stratum reserved for the 'show-offs', a rung of the ladder that it is almost impossible to ever recover from.

What the IADF – and circus in general – revealed to me was twofold.

Firstly, that expression is an important form of self-development; it can be a method of holding a conversation with yourself about who you are, what you are, and how that might grow. Secondly, it provided the realisation that performance does not occur solely on a stage in an arts context, but is present across our social landscape. Playing football was a performance. I went out in front of an audience, I replicated the routines I had learned in training, and I attempted to execute them as well as I could in hopes of taking the drama of competition and casting myself into the role of victor. But win or lose, I was performing, and so were the team.

It was simply that the pitch was a stage, and I'd been a performer my whole life, just within a competitive context rather than an artistic one.

This realisation was liberating, because it removed the principal barrier that existed between me and this new world, which was one of my own construction anyway. It gave me permission to explore it without a sense of fear that I might be doing something I shouldn't.

Of course, I would come to feel like an impostor again, many times, and still do to this day, but this was a realisation that had to solidify itself into my mentality over time, via a series of continual reinforcements. Just like anything I would have ever done in football, I had to train myself into believing it.

And, on top of all that, the IADF was where I first discovered the cyr wheel.

From the off, the wheel suited me better than the other apparatuses. It was the one most forgiving to my method of trying to force things out without any sense of grace or any regard for the well-being of the people around me. It was also the one that seemed the newest and most exciting. Every other piece of circus apparatus – rope, silks, trapeze, harness – already had a sizeable cohort of Irish people practising it.

As coincidence would have it, that summer of 2013 was the first time the cyr wheel had been included in the IADF programme. It meant that I came to it with a smaller, less experienced group of people around me, which allowed me the confidence to put myself forward without the fear of being made to look foolish by someone far more advanced. The people I studied with were people I could look at and think, I can do that as well.

It's definitely an arrogance on my part, but throughout my life I've continuously found myself in positions where I have watched another person accomplish a particular skill or feat and immediately felt the drive to either replicate or better their display. If they can do it, so can I, I would say to myself. And, what was more, maybe I could do it better.

It's partly what made me a decent competitor. It's also what led me into trying so many different things, of which the wheel would eventually become the most dominant.

Later, I would also identify the wheel as a gap in the Irish performance market. With so few male aerialists, and even fewer wheel performers, I would potentially stand a better chance of making something of myself as a performer if I had the wheel under my belt as my artistic weapon of choice.

Those two weeks in June 2013 were a fantastic experience, fuelling me with the desire to continue improving with this circus thing.

Come the autumn I was due back for football, back to Elphin to play for my club, with a return to the county panel scheduled for beyond that again, but more and more that seemed an unattractive prospect to me.

Despite my misgivings, this was still what I intended to do. However, my mental effort was increasingly devoted not towards reclaiming my previous level of footballing ability, but towards figuring out how I might include circus and the cyr wheel into my daily life alongside my other commitments.

What I needed first was a wheel of my own.

The circus world is a small one. Even sectoral superstars are well within reach. It's a bit like the GAA that way: a loose community of disparate people linked by a common bond. Which is how, one day, I found myself talking to Daniel Cyr, the inventor of the cyr wheel.

I'd found his number online by doing something that seemed far too simple to contact a man of his stature, which was hammering his name into a search engine and trawling the first few results.

It turned out that Daniel wasn't only a performer, but he made cyr wheels as well. Of course, he had to. He'd invented them. When he was originally developing the apparatus, he'd had no one else to turn to for experience; he'd had to figure it out as he went. If he didn't make them, there was no one else who could.

I'd spent a few weeks staring at his number, psyching myself up to call him before psyching myself out again. I wanted to order a wheel, and even though I was a complete amateur, I thought getting one straight from the inventor sounded pretty cool. I reasoned that, if nothing else, the aura from a hand-crafted, Cyr-original wheel would lend me an air of authenticity that could be helpful in covering for my still-developing level of skill.

But the idea of ringing someone in his position just *seemed* wrong. I mean, why should I be allowed to talk to, and potentially order from, a wheel master when I was little more than a beginner enthusiast who was still only doing this thing as a hobby? Still, I ultimately plucked up the courage and got him on the phone.

He was a lovely man. One of those chilled French-Canadian people who don't seem capable of a different mode of conversation other than a slow-drawled dreaminess. He would have been happy to build me a wheel, he said, but he was heading away on tour and he just didn't think he'd have the time. (Of course he was, I said to myself. He was a real person; a real performer. He did this for a living.)

But hope was not lost. There was another crowd based in Germany that I could try. Or, and here was an idea, maybe I could just make one myself.

I was, after all, a practical sort. I had studied education through metalwork in university while most of my mates there had been woodworkers. I understood the fundamentals of metal design, and a cyr wheel was a relatively simple piece of kit, a hollow metal circle made from either steel or aluminium, divided into parts and fitted together with small, in-line, Allen-head bolt fixings.

After some advice from Daniel, I decided to just go for it.

I figured that for a man of my height and build I would need a wheel with a circumference of about six metres. I contacted Patterson Ring Rolling in Belfast and told them my requirements. They rolled me out two lengths of hollow aluminium, enough to make two wheels since I had anticipated making a balls of my first effort, and a third length that was just small enough to fit inside the large ones, so I could fashion the sections of the wheel into male/female style connectors, where one end slots into the other.

Once the lengths of aluminium arrived, I cut, shaped and fitted them myself, using the engineering room in the secondary school where I worked. I finished it off by covering the aluminium in a skin of black rubber food-grade hosepipe. This covering would make the wheel easier to work with, giving traction to its surface while also delivering some protection to the surfaces on which I intended to use it.

It's a great thing to be a little bit handy. I've always had an appreciation for it, and I understand what a shame it is for people who never get the opportunity to learn some form of working with their hands. There's a lot of schools who look down on things like metalwork or woodwork, as they are considered classes into which the academically disadvantaged can be herded and kept occupied. It doesn't help when we have an educational system that privileges points-gathering over aptitude. And that type of snobbery is one that perpetuates itself, which makes things worse. It's a shame. There's a great sense of pride and accomplishment, never mind practical benefit, to be gained from being able to craft something yourself.

With my wheel secured, I began figuring out a way of continuing to train while I was still working and training for football.

Those years of 2013/14 were still very much post-recession, austerity-heavy times in Ireland, which had very few benefits at all, save for this: being still considered as a junior-level teacher, having only qualified three years previously, meant that my regular contract was for just eight teaching hours a week, as opposed to the twenty-two that made up a full-time and permanent position. This meant that I had plenty of free periods and spare time during my normal working week, which, in turn, meant I could bring my wheel to school and continue to train.

In the gaps between teaching, I would take myself off to the school hall, a gym space with lacquered wooden floors and lots of space, and spend my time honing the lessons I'd been taught in Donegal, while attempting to figure new things out through a mixture of my own ingenuity and studying videos of other people online.

That's the way with circus. Tricks, such as they are, become public property once they are put out into the world. If you can figure out how to do it, then you can add it to your repertoire, and this was something I was eager to do.

I was also lucky to find, now that I had opened myself up to the possibility of it, that an increasing number of opportunities to do new and exciting performance-related things were presenting themselves to me.

In the six months between that first IADF and the Christmas of that year I was asked to do a number of small gigs with Fidget Feet, who had quickly come to appropriate me as their own once I had demonstrated a willingness to do pretty much whatever they asked of me, such as acting as a counterweight during the development of their new show, *The Second Coming*, a Yeats-inspired fusion of aerial dance and traditional Irish arts.

I was also lucky that Shane Holohan had managed to convince a few top-quality performers to come to Carrick-on-Shannon to deliver workshops, including the Belfast-based Tumble Circus, a manic collection of circus-heads who specialise in creating hilariously political productions. They opened my eyes further still to the possibilities that were available to me within this new world.

I continued to work like that throughout the year, taking any chance and any opportunity available to me.

Behind this, football began to creep back in. The Roscommon county panel were due to reconvene and, as I was coming towards the end of my year out from the sport, I got a phone call from one of the selectors inviting me to rejoin the squad.

This was a phone call that I had been expecting. It was also one I had come to dread, because the once-creeping thought of not wanting to return to my previous modes of operation, my micro-focused attitude to training and the achievement of marginal gains, had firmly taken root. I liked not having my life determined by the successes and failures of the footballing season. I liked not heaping pressure upon myself or the people around me, my teammates and family. I liked being able to enjoy myself again.

When the call came I had already decided to put things off for a while. I told the selector that I wanted to go back playing club first for a bit. I was still only finding my fitness again and I wanted to be able to build up my confidence from within the safety of a club setting. The selector understood this all perfectly well.

No bother at all, he said to me. Only, don't leave it too long before giving us a shout. You'd not want to lose your place on the county panel.

The warning was clear. Their tolerance with my truancy from football was nearing its end. Sooner or later, I'd need to either show up or ship out. Which was completely understandable. I'd have been no different in their position. But even then, I was increasingly certain that I wouldn't be back.

To get players into the sport, you need to influence them away from any competing interests – like soccer or computers or pubs or life. You have to get them into the team structure while they're young – preferably for Under–8s at the very least – and then you've got to keep them there.

It's not uncommon to get selectors and 'good club men' dropping into homes, schools or workplaces to chase up players for every conceivable age level of competition, all in an effort to keep on track those who might stray away from the GAA doctrine.

It's impossible not to lose players. The time commitment can often be far too onerous for balanced people to burden themselves with, even when they have the talent. But there is a vast structure of people there to try and limit the losses as much as possible. It goes far beyond just the core club and county management. It's a cross-community network in which it can sometimes seem like everyone you know is involved.

It's the comments from teachers during school, or from the parents of your friends outside of that.

How are you set for the match? When are you back to the club?

It's the idle conversation when you're at work or at home.

They lost it in the second half. Ran out of gas. They could have done with you out there.

It's the sidelong looks and muffled talk when you walk into a shop or pop into a pub.

There he is. Meant to be injured. Looks fine to me. Enjoying himself, it seems.

It builds up all around you into a siege of pressure.

You are coming back though, aren't you? Sure, what else would you be doing? And doesn't your club need you?

And aside from all that, there's the pressure of expectation and duty that you heap onto yourself. You feel obliged to make yourself available to the club and to the county. You've worked hard for it, certainly, so there's an element of not wanting to put that work to waste. But there's also this sense of opportunity being granted to you above so many others, which seems just plain ungrateful to spurn.

There are so many people that dream of playing for the first team of their club, and more again who dream of being selected for the county panel. It's the stuff of childhood fantasy. There's no way around that. So, when you find yourself considering packing it all in, it can be a decision that is hard to make peace with.

That the reality of the situation is so different, so much more all-consuming than you might ever have imagined, doesn't seem to justify the fact that you've been given a golden ticket, coveted by thousands, tens of thousands of people across the country, and you're potentially going to say no.

There's also a more conventional wisdom that comes into play. The idea that if you're good at something then you should do that thing, whatever it might be, and regardless of whether you enjoy it or not. It's that kind of thinking that traps people in careers they don't like. Their interests don't come into it.

That idea of waste and expectation is so pernicious when it comes to life choices. It puts people the world over into situations that are stressful and demotivating and can, potentially, make them very unhappy.

The enjoyment had gone from my football, but my skill level, injuries notwithstanding, was still high enough to compete at a senior level. That I was still good enough was the only thing that people considered. I was fit enough, I was good enough, I should go and play. Simple as that.

And let's be clear, less than twelve months previously, I would have had exactly the same mindset. Never once did I really stop to consider the other things that might be going on in people's lives, the million little challenges that we all struggle with as we make our way through the world: holding down a job, not having a job, getting a job; finding a partner, keeping a partner, leaving a partner; babies, houses, pets, grief, loss, joy, discovery and everything else in between. I didn't consider that. I just saw a player, devoid of their context to the world beyond football. Only a player who needed to play the game better and commit themselves to the cause more.

Like I was doing.

Like I had done.

It wasn't healthy, and I now realised that I had begun to change.

***

Working on my own with the wheel in the free moments I managed to carve out for myself at school and in the evenings became an exhilarating process. One of the things I came to enjoy the most was the self-determination of it.

The wheel did what I told it to do, nothing else. If it crashed to the floor, or slammed into my shin, it did that for no other reason than I had unwittingly made it do that. The better I got at controlling it, then the more I could get it to do what I wanted. There was no one else involved in this equation; there was only me. As for what I wanted to achieve, and how far I was willing to go, no one else had any say in that. No one else had any expectations.

Team sports, and even a lot of so-called individual sports, are really a complex weave of different people feeding into the process in different ways and at different times. They all have their roles to play, and any one of them not performing to their capacity has a knock-on negative effect on the team and, consequently, your own performance. It means that even with the best will in the world, even when you are controlling the controllable within your own small sphere of influence, your fate is largely in the hands of the people around you. It's not a flaw of the system, it's just the nature of the game.

But learning with the wheel was a guilt-free experience that I found so freeing. If I didn't train, I wasn't letting anyone down but myself. If I didn't complete a trick on my first hundred goes, then it didn't matter, because I had as long as I needed to figure it out. I had the permission to steer my own ship however I pleased, picking my own course from a broad and undiscovered horizon. The result of this was that I slowly realised that I wanted to follow this course very far.

Much further than I had ever suspected, and way beyond what anyone else might have ever imagined.

So, when I did come back to my club footballing life with the Elphin team, I did so in a much more relaxed manner. I was no longer unrelentingly demanding. I didn't seek the county level of commitment from my fellow club players. I didn't heap that sort of pressure upon them. I began to realise how unrealistic and unfair that was. I began to look at these players as people, understanding that there were other things they all had going on. And that was okay. More even. That was good.

Of course, this did not go unnoticed by either the Elphin management team or the vast community network of passionate football people that surrounded the club. They spotted my priorities changing; my approach softening. They saw me slowly drifting away. And they immediately kicked things into gear to try and bring me back to focus, to set me back on track.

During that season back with Elphin, I was given the captaincy of the team. I was a senior player for the club. I was one of the best performers. That was all true, and it was an honour, without a doubt. But the message beyond that was still clear to see. Let's give this lad the captaincy to peg him down. He's in danger of slacking off. As captain he'll have a duty to the club that he can't shirk. He'll have to knuckle down. He'll have to recommit.

Again, I can't blame them for that. They were right, after all. I wasn't like I had been previously. My edge came from my competitiveness, my energy and my devotion as much as it did from my skill. If any of that began to fade, then I would lose my grip on the player I had been before and the player I could be again.

In addition to this, there was the Elphin GAA Club anniversary. To celebrate their one-hundred and twenty-fifth year of existence, they had decided to select an All-Star team made up of players who had played for Elphin over the last thirty-five years (the rationale there being that it would be much more of an event if the players selected as All-Stars were still around to enjoy it). We'd had a lot of good players, and I was told that I was in with a really good shout of making the All-Star selection.

Outside of Elphin, this idea might have meant nothing at all. I'm sure it doesn't to you. I'm sure it all seems a little bit quaint and rural. But from within the community, this was a massive deal. I cannot overstate it; it was huge. The whole identity of the Elphin community was so closely intertwined with the history of the club, it would have been impossible to conceive of one without the other. And to be in consideration for selection was genuinely an honour. No glibness. No qualifications. It was an honour.

When I set to thinking about this All-Star situation, there were two schools of thought competing inside of me. There was the Irish side of me that said of course I didn't warrant a selection, and it was embarrassing to even think of it. But there was the competitive side of me that said, hang on a second, I'm in with a good shout here, and if I get selected it's because I deserve it, and do you know what, I think I might actually deserve this.

The night was organised as a gala dinner, with the great and good from the club and the community all invited to attend. Aidan O'Mahony, the Kerry All-Star, was even presenting the awards. Imagine a country wedding taking place in the windowless function room of the local hotel, all white tablecloths, purple uplighting and seldom-worn suits. It was that. None of the players in attendance had been told whether or not they had been selected, so I went with no idea as to whether or not I'd make it.

When my name was called out as one of the fifteen players selected, I will not lie, the swell of pride, achievement and recognition was immense. I was honoured to have been picked alongside the others who made the All-Star team. It meant so much to me to be thought of in those terms by the people I loved and grew up with. I was delighted, and it remains one of my proudest moments to this day, but it was infused and, in some ways, tainted by my increasing certainty that my footballing days were numbered. I couldn't shake the feeling that I was betraying the good faith of everyone in attendance at that celebration of Elphin football.

This award wasn't another piece of leverage designed by the club management to get me to stay. I'm not saying that. No. It was a recognition of what I had achieved. And yet, being fit and having the goodwill and appreciation of everyone there so publicly displayed, I found myself fractured between my pride and my guilt. If I left, I was going to let these people down.

My pride from that award is undimmed. And I've made peace with the guilt.

Mostly.

The season continued and, as far as the management was concerned, my attitude did not improve. In fact, it got worse. I had not lost my ability, but I was no longer a dead certainty for every training session. And now there were even some matches I was missing. This meant that, captaincy or no, there were times when I was not guaranteed my place in the starting fifteen.

It came to a head during the summer of 2014. The Irish Aerial Dance Fest in Donegal had come around again and I was going again, football or no. Try explaining that to a group of middle-aged, Roscommon football men: *Sorry, but there's this circus thing – well, aerial circus thing – happening in Donegal that I'm going to. No, it's not for work (not yet, anyway, I say to myself). No. It's not like a big-top circus with clowns and animals and that. It's in the air. Trapezes and stuff. Although there's stuff on the ground that I'm into as well. Wheels. But anyway. I'm going and it means I'll miss training. I know I'm the captain. I know that. But this only happens once a year and so ... Yes. I know there's a fixture right in the middle of those two weeks. I'll travel back down for that. But no, I won't make the trainings. And yes. I will be gone.*

I'd actually already booked a month-long course with Aisling Ní Cheallaigh, my performance partner, for the month of August. I had met Aisling in 2012 at the *Taking Flight* weekend workshops in Carrick-on-Shannon that

Shane Holohan had used to organise, where I had first encountered circus. She was already further on in her circus career development at this point, but she'd been looking to do more doubles work, like doubles trapeze and doubles floor acrobatics. It just so happened that I'd come along at the right time and that we hit it off. I'd been training with her intermittently ever since and we'd found that we worked really well together, complementing each other's performing styles while sharing a similar sense of humour.

The course would take place in the École de cirque de Québec. It was an amazing opportunity to see whether or not I had what it took, whether it was worth Aisling and myself working together as a duo, and to figure out whether or not I might not want to give this circus thing a proper go. But that landed right in the middle of the prime championship fixtures for the club. Once again, it meant that I wouldn't be there. But I didn't tell the club management that. I didn't have it in me to fight that battle right then. Best off to lead them into this slowly, I thought.

That they were unimpressed with my decision to abscond to Donegal was evident to us all. This wasn't the behaviour of a fully committed senior player, nor of a club captain. I had agreed to travel back down for the match we had against Boyle, which was scheduled for the middle of the IADF, but I was becoming fairly certain that they were bringing me down to make an example of me, to send a clear and unequivocal message that their patience was at an end, and that, regardless of form or ability, I would find myself riding the bench.

Leaving Letterkenny during the festival was a nightmare in and of itself, as it meant I had to walk out in the middle of a whole pile of things. I had been given an opportunity to perform on my own for the first time during one of the IADF's performance nights. It was going to be a simple piece of silks with my brother playing guitar as accompaniment, but it was a huge deal for me. I was putting myself right out there and saying: this is a real thing. There were also classes I would be missing, and I would be letting down a few other folks whom I'd promised to help with their own IADF performances.

In addition to all that, Fidget Feet had a special third week planned for a select group of people to work together underneath the guidance of Charlie Morrissey, a hugely experienced director and creator of outdoor spectacle work. It was an opportunity to learn from him about what it took to enter into the creative process for a non-theatre-style venue.

I had been invited to take part in this week, which would culminate in the performance of a specially created show taking place against the backdrop of the beautiful Ards Friary, with the panoramic Lough Swilly wrapped around it. It was a huge honour and a big opportunity, one which I needed to prep for.

But I was leaving.

I made the two-hour-plus drive from Letterkenny to Croghan, fully expecting but not entirely believing that, for the first time in my club life, I could be on the bench. I couldn't blame them. From their point of view, they were absolutely right to put me on the bench. I wasn't committed. I hadn't been training. I didn't deserve it.

But I had made the starting line-up for almost every sporting thing I had ever attempted since before I was in school. I'd been good enough to compete at Mosney in the junior athletic competitions for sprint running. I'd made, of all things, a trampoline team organised by the very same Shane Holohan who would later introduce me to circus.

It meant that I actually didn't know how to be a substitute. Fair enough, at county level I'd had to sit on the bench just like everyone else, but here, at club, it was different. What was I supposed to do? Should I just sit there, take my scolding and do nothing? Should I be animated and energetic on the sideline? Should I try and give advice and encouragement, or was that only the coaches' role? I didn't know.

But I was getting ahead of myself. The team hadn't been named yet. I didn't know where I was.

I soon found out.

I landed down into Croghan for the match. In the dressing room, the number twenty-three jersey was tossed over to me. It was official, I was to be a substitute.

All my actions had brought things to here, and there was no escaping it any longer.

We togged out, warmed up and the match began. From there, it was an absolute disaster.

We were trying to employ a new defensive system that we didn't know well enough and we got exposed, repeatedly. Our discipline was all over the shop and we ended up with only twelve men on the pitch as opposed to fifteen. We lost by 3–10 to 1–5. And I didn't come on during the entire game. I wanted to be on. I knew that I was good enough to be on. I think the management and the players knew that too. We would have been better for having me on there. Which is not to say that we wouldn't have lost. Who knows? But it definitely wouldn't have been as bad.

On the other hand, did I deserve to be on? No. Probably not.

And there was another thing. By trying to please everyone, by trying to juggle a footballing life with my growing interest and commitment to this circus thing, I was only letting everyone down. I had let my football team down by not being there for training. I was their captain and I wasn't there. But I had also let down the circus folk in Letterkenny. I had committed to helping people with their shows, to performing myself, and I was doing none of that any justice either.

I was spreading myself way too thin. I needed to make a decision for the sake of everyone involved.

If I wasn't going to pursue football anymore, then for the sake of myself and the team, I just needed to come clean about it. Regardless of best intentions, by continuing on in this half-limbo existence, I was hurting them, and I was hurting myself.

I had to make the choice of football or circus. And so, I did.

I never again wore an Elphin jersey.

I cherish my time as a footballer: the things I accomplished, the friends I made, the experiences I had. But I do not regret leaving it behind. I never have. That phase of my life was now over.

NINE

BULLY TO YOU

(Teenage angst masking adult anger, the sordid underbelly of being a jock, an incalculable maze and the worries that the future brings.)

There's something that we've been dancing around for a while now. It's popped up throughout this story so far: in the Bellanagare disco, in the GAA, in *Riot*, and I think it's time to come clean and just say it straight.

In my younger years I could be a bit of an ass and definitely had the ability to bully.

No.

That's not plain enough.

Spit it out, Ronan. Just spit it out.

Okay. Here goes.

I was a bully.

In school, from my youth until the later end of secondary school, I was a bully.

It's not something I'm proud of. I don't like thinking about myself in those terms because I wasn't *only* a bully, I was also kind and funny and driven and loyal. But the truth remains. I was all of those things, and I was also a bully. One thing does not preclude the other, but it does not excuse it either.

I was a bully. I was then, and I have the capacity and potential to be again, should I ever choose.

There, I said it.

No, I don't feel better. But that's not the point of this.

Why was I a bully? There are many reasons for that. Partly, it was the small-town culture, living in a village where there's only the GAA rising up like a monolith to the exclusion of anything else. There's the privilege of your reputation as an athlete and as a man, a set of social positions which demand a very strict code of conduct in order to be maintained. And then there's also anger, bubbling away beneath it all.

But anger at what?

We'll come to that.

When you're angry there's a very easy way to deal with it. You displace it. You decide that you can make yourself feel better by making someone else feel worse. It's a terrible model, destructive and ultimately futile, but it's an extremely seductive one. Why? That's simple, really. It's because it's so goddamn easy to access. Especially when you come from a majority grouping like I did.

It's easy to bully people who are different because, assuming you are 'normal', their difference puts them in a minority and minorities are easier to oppress. They're less likely to have someone around to stand up for them, while it's very likely that you, in your dominant position, will have someone to back you up, regardless of how wrong or how out of line you might be.

Being part of the group always trumps being right or wrong. It's something that's very obvious in our politics at the moment, and it's the story of our human existence.

I wasn't the sort of bully who would plan things out. I wasn't the type to go out and punch someone in the face out of the blue. Nor did I have a sustained target for my aggressions. There wasn't one puny kid who bore the brunt of my dominion. But all the same, I was very adept at making other people feel small.

My preferred method of bullying was much more opportunistic in nature. It meant that I subjected a wide range of people to my behaviour as individual incidents. This had a benefit. It made my actions a lot easier to rationalise. I could dress them up as having the craic. I could dismiss it as being just fun between myself and my mates, which of course made it a lot easier to hide the reality from myself, because I didn't think of myself as a bully until I was much older. Bullies were pricks, and I didn't think of myself as a prick. If you got offended or hurt by something I did, then that was *your* fault. *You* were taking things too seriously. *You* were the one who needed to lighten up.

Like this one time that myself and a mate were messing around with a basketball after school. I had neither the plan nor the intention to hurt anyone doing this, but just as I was about to put my boot through the basketball and volley it to the other side of the court for no other reason than it would annoy my friend, I spotted that one of my other classmates was just about to cross my strike-path. So, instead of kicking the ball away, I kicked it at him. I put every ounce of power I could muster into that kick, sending the ball hurtling towards him at such a tremendous velocity that even I was impressed by it.

When it struck him square in the face, I was surprised. I hadn't meant that, I'd just meant to hit him in general. When it turned out that the force of the kick had managed to shatter the poor fellow's glasses right off his face, it only made things funnier. I didn't really appreciate how small and vulnerable I'd made this person feel. I'd just done it for a laugh, I hadn't really meant to do lasting damage. But that didn't change the fact that I had.

At the time, I got into trouble for that. So much so that myself and my mate had to buy a replacement pair of glasses for the victim. I feel terrible about it now. But that was the sort of person I was back then.

There were plenty of other examples of this.

Any Irish person of my generation will remember how ludicrously heavy our school backpacks used to be. Daily we would carry our own personal library of workbooks to and from the school. We were basically student sherpas.

Our school was an amalgamation of the tech and the grammar school, so we used both buildings. We would often be timetabled in the other school after lunch, depending on what classes we had. This meant that many of us would leave our bags at the school gates at lunch rather than carting them from one end of Elphin to the other; a small mountain of school bags left unattended and vulnerable to those looking to make trouble. On this one occasion, beside the mountain of bags, some concrete blocks had been left over by workmen who had been redoing the school gates, and I happened to find myself presented with an irresistible opportunity to cause some mayhem. Before me was the backpack of possibly the kindest girl in school, and beside that, just by coincidence, was a concrete block. The idea I came up with wasn't complicated. I was going to put the concrete block into her bag. Hilarious, no? She would have to lug this heavier-than-usual millstone all the way to class, and when she opened it up to get her books, she'd find a dirty great big concrete block in there instead. Genius.

I removed most of her books from her bag to make room for the block, placing the unneeded books into my own bag so I could return them after the prank since I was, after all, a considerate bully. I kept a few of her books in her bag as bookends so as not to give the game away. The bag prepped, I retreated to a safe distance to survey my work.

Things didn't go quite to plan. When this poor girl tried to pick up the bag, the block was so heavy that it ripped straight through the bag, causing it to practically explode from the seams.

Some form of guilt was almost immediate, and I went to help her. Together we gathered up her books and walked, in tense silence, to the other school building. All the while I was internally cursing the quality of her bag for spoiling the joke. I was late for my own class because of this, and I even legitimised my lateness by explaining to the teacher that I had been helping someone carry their books! What a hero I was.

I got in trouble for that one too, another example of my destruction requiring the purchase of replacement articles by way of reconciliation. But it didn't stop me. I did this kind of thing again and again. I wasn't sorry. Not until much, much later.

In other words, I was frequently a right prick.

A lot of this dickish, cocky arsebaggery came directly from my success at sport. It provided me with a rationale, but this is not a justification. I was angry and I was looking for avenues in which to express that.

My football career not only gave me an outlet; it actually placed me in a set of circumstances that actively encouraged my aggression. I've talked before about my reputation for having controlled aggression on the football field. It was an attribute that was lauded by various coaches because it meant that I was a fierce competitor, willing to put everything out there for the sake of the result.

That was great for everyone invested in the club. The team would be stronger, and I would be given the opportunity to vent. But it was a scenario that meant, for all intents and purposes, I was a bully on the pitch as well as off it, which did nothing to disincentivise my behaviour.

Often, I would target someone on the pitch. It might have been someone who had angered me, or it might have been just because I was angry.

It was rationalised under the guise of competition, but wasn't it just another version of making someone else feel bad in order to make myself feel better? There it was, this cycle of anger within me that was been released without being treated.

The fighting in the discos and clubs we visited as teenagers, and our disputes with the townies were other examples of this anger being vented. The wayward anger in there is impossible to ignore. It wasn't just seeking excuses to lash out, it was inventing them as well.

Why all this anger? Where on earth was it coming from?

In many ways, it was typical teenage confusion, a maelstrom of testosterone and other hormones that would give you a no-reason-boner one second followed by a furious anger the next. But that wasn't all it was. It can't have been. Not every footballer went into their games looking to hurt someone. Not every teenager went to the discos on the lookout for a fight.

No. Let's be honest, shall we? My anger was coming from somewhere very real and very personal, but it was being channelled ever outwards towards the unfortunate souls within my social or sporting orbit.

My anger was coming from what was happening within my family – because it was slowly falling apart.

***

'All happy families are alike; each unhappy family is unhappy in its own way.'

A smart man wrote that a long time ago. And it's an easy one to misunderstand. At least I think it is. Because it's not an idea that's intended as a binary; one does not preclude the other. An unhappy family isn't only unhappy and vice versa.

No. It's that happiness has a common root, while unhappiness is always individual.

In most cases, what you would call a 'normal' family is in

fact a hybrid mixture of both. Happy and unhappy, often in the same moment, because life, emotion and experience resist binary positions.

My family were no different, mired as they were within the complex repressions and societal gymnastics forced upon them by a rural Irish backdrop still deeply indentured to the Catholic Church. For instance, my parents had their children young. They had seven by the time they were twenty-seven.

The first, my older sister Kate, was born before my parents were married, when they were twenty and nineteen respectively. That's an early age to have a child by any standard, but in early eighties Roscommon, this was still considered something of a potential scandal that had to be handled delicately lest shame be brought upon the family.

Mammy, who had just begun her second year of college, went off to Galway to live with her brother, finish the course, see out the pregnancy and give birth. When she returned, she did so without Kate in her arms. There was no danger of Mammy being whisked off to a Magdalene Laundry, but having a child before being married carried with it a certain level of judgement in Ireland in the late eighties, so keeping Kate a secret was a prudent move while Mammy and Daddy figured out whether they should get married and keep her, or if she should be given up for adoption.

After the birth in June, my parents quickly decided to marry and keep Kate, with the wedding set for October. This didn't mean that Kate was retrieved right away, however. It was still felt that it wouldn't be right for her to return until the nuptials were firmly settled, so for the first four months of her life, my sister Kate lived in a convent that my parents visited regularly.

This was the sort of thing my parents grew up with. As much as the rigid rule of conservative Catholicism has receded in this country over the last thirty years, it was still a hugely influential factor in how my family learned to live its life.

My parents moved around a bit in the early years, spending some time in Dublin, which is where I was born, then heading to Ballina for work when I was two, before eventually returning to Roscommon when I was four to take over my father's family farm.

Moving there was great for us as children. It put us in a rural environment with the freedom of movement and action that I've talked about previously. The school was less than two miles away and we could walk in and out to that if we weren't given a lift. It also put the extended Brady family on our doorstep; a wide coterie of aunts, uncles and cousins from around the area, providing us with a huge selection of people to play with.

It also gave us that particular brand of country colour that we loved. Like Pat Harrington and his donkey and trap. We'd frequently pass Pat on our way in to school or the football pitch. He'd be sat on his trap with a donkey about as old as Egypt pulling him along the road. He'd always offer a lift, but we could walk faster than his donkey could pull, and besides, the poor animal didn't need us adding to his burdens, so we'd politely decline and pass Pat out. Pat was generally on his way to the bog or checking cattle, but sometimes he'd be going to the pub. He would park the donkey outside and proceed to drink and socialise with all the other locals in what was often the only social outlet in rural Ireland (except mass on Sundays of course). Pat wasn't one to drink and drive, so when he'd had his fill, he would amble outside and plonk himself down onto the back of the trap. He was in safe hooves though, because the donkey knew exactly what to do. In that quiet and unhurried way it had, the donkey would simply turn for home and carry its master with it. They were an old couple, and when the old donkey finally died, Pat wasn't far behind, neither being really able to live without the other.

That story is bittersweet, but it was this kind of character-driven life we loved as children, so moving home was a revelation for us. It also meant we could attend more family gatherings, of which there were many.

Some people hate family gatherings, but the Brady clan live for them. They're fantastic craic. Even the funerals are cherished events that any of us are loathe to miss. I get really sad when I miss a big gathering, and football made me miss a lot of these events. As youngsters, we didn't understand that the prodigious size of the extended Brady family was slightly unusual even by Irish standards.

But, similarly, we didn't understand what a strain moving home put on my parents, because Roscommon was a small place with many broken people living in it, and the Brady farm was no different.

The farm I grew up on, the same one where Cleo would

later drag me around a field, was in Corrigeen, two miles from Bellanagare village and seven miles from Elphin. Grandad Brady lived on the farm with various uncles surrounding it in the usual country fashion. Granny Brady lived eight miles away in Tulsk for reasons that I'll come to. My mother's parents, Grandad and Nanny Dowd, were based in Moneylea, which in turn was five miles away from Corrigeen.

Moving home meant that we all piled in on top of an already convoluted mess of expectations, grudges and struggles, bringing our own rapidly expanding complications to bear as well.

Mammy was a civil servant and, despite giving birth to seven children, she remained the primary breadwinner for the family over the years. She was and is a formidably loving woman who rarely raises her voice (although she can if required), but has the stoic command of authority that comes from having lived a life that forced her quickly into adulthood.

Dad worked the farm upon our return, taking over from Grandad Brady and one of my dad's brothers. Grandad still lived with us after Dad took over, which had its own complications, as a farm is never completely handed over while the previous owner is still very much present. Irish farms are rarely rich ventures; they require a lot of money to keep running, and work to very tight and ever-dwindling margins. They demand almost constant attention, especially when they are based around livestock, like the Brady farm.

The stereotypical image of the farmer is that of a person who rises before dawn, when the chill still clings to the air, works through the day, and is early to bed. For many farmers, this is exactly the truth. When there aren't animals to feed, to separate, to move, to tend to, there are other things that need attention: boundaries to be mended, feed to be collected, machinery to be maintained, jobs that breed other jobs, like mushrooms in the dark, and that ignores the paperwork, of which there is an ever-increasing amount for your stock or your grants or your loans or your insurance and what have you.

My dad was not a stereotypical farmer. Our farm required the same amount of attention, of course, but by the time I was in secondary school, my dad was a man who always seemed to sleep a lot.

This was especially apparent during the summer months, when all us kids would be milling about the farmhouse on our summer holidays, wasting time and generally idling in that wonderful boredom you only get when you're too young to appreciate it.

Mammy would leave early for her job as a civil servant in the department of education and we would be left to potter around to our own devices. Dad would be there, and officially speaking he was supposed to be up, tending to the farm and keeping an eye on us, but that would rarely occur. More usually, Dad would sleep late, staying hidden in his bedroom until well into the morning, maybe even as far as lunch.

We were always delighted to see him, because when he did arise, it meant we were in for some fun. The farm work was never so pressing as to prevent him from coming into the field and playing with us, messing around with a football or wrestling or whatever it might have been at the time.

It was great, especially as we got a little older and started playing proper matches, because Dad would play with us, in what felt like exhilarating full throttle, although somehow I imagine he must have been keeping something back. He would have been late twenties into early thirties, and still in what would pass for the best shape of his life.

Those days became golden, full of sweat and the smell of soil from our full-contact sporting endeavours. We loved them. But no work ever got done.

More often than not, Mammy would have left a list of jobs that needed attending to around the house, which should have stood beside the work required on the farm anyway. As the day slowly dripped away from late morning to late afternoon, the spectre of her impending return would rise over us and a mild panic eventually took hold. For an indeterminate period of time prior to her arrival there would be a rush to try and make it look like we'd at least attempted some of the jobs. It was always slapdash and, unlike in the family football matches that we had lavished in during the day, we never fully committed.

She would return to find the farm and the house up in a heap, which was inevitable given the lack of care that had been shown towards either of them. This would cause her to get angry, which would make us feel a little bad, but mostly it would breed a sense of resentfulness towards her as an impossible ogre trying to unjustly stamp her foot on our harmless fun.

For a while, Mammy became the villain to us. How could she not? It wasn't a fair fight when Dad was occupying all the super-fun territory. We weren't old enough to appreciate that the neglect shown on his part was forcing Mammy into this role. We only saw a cranky battle-axe returning at the end of the day to squash us versus a sparkling wizard of entertainment who was simply interested in granting us a good time.

This did absolutely nothing for the welfare of the farm or the strength of the family finances, heaping ever more pressure on Mammy to deliver as the sole breadwinner, which in turn did nothing to aid the health of my parents' relationship.

It took a while, but even as children we eventually began to become frustrated with Dad's lethargy that, given long enough, seemed to creep up around everything, including his inclination to amuse us.

In true childish fashion, this was initially because we were forced into taking up the slack for all the farm work that he wasn't doing. This pissed us off. We didn't want to work. We wanted to play. But we also didn't think of the farm as 'ours'. It always seemed more like 'his'. He was the one who had chosen to return to it. He was the one who had decided to take over the running of it. He was the one who was refusing to tend to it. Yet we were the ones being saddled with paying the price for his neglect.

In our sullen self-interest, we would end up half-assing a lot of the jobs. This would get us in trouble, which would make us angry and resentful and more likely to half-ass things again by way of retaliation. And so, the cycle continued, forever downwards for everyone involved, breeding a sense of bitterness that became a palpable residence in the farmhouse.

From this lofty position of hindsight, where compassion is a much easier feeling to generate, I'm sure it wasn't easy for him. I say that he *wanted* to return to the farm, that he brought the family back to Roscommon because he *wanted* to run it and thought he could make a success of it, but I don't think that's really true. It was a family farm, and I'm not sure he saw much choice in the matter, with an ever-expanding young family and no qualifications or trade.

Dad had a father too, Grandad Brady, a man who rarely, if ever at all, had a good word to say about his son.

Grandad Brady loved my dad. I don't doubt that. But he hadn't the words for that kind of emotion. The only words he had, the only methods of communicating he had access to, were ones of negativity and criticism. That wouldn't have been an uncommon trait for the time and I imagine Grandad Brady was raised the same way when he was a child.

Either way, it meant that whatever Dad did, it always seemed to be wrong. He could attempt and complete something, but it was never good enough or was never done correctly, not how Grandad Brady would have done it.

Which was strange, since Grandad Brady had no problem defending my dad when he wasn't around. If we ever complained about Dad's sleeping or irritability, Grandad would leap to his defence; the man isn't well, he'd say. He's sick. It would be similar if people outside the family criticised Dad. Grandad Brady wouldn't stand for it. He just didn't seem to be able to tell his son that. It was as if when he saw Dad, all his caring words dried up and only criticism came out. I'm sure he thought he was doing right by his son, but that sort of thing would sap anyone, robbing you of care or motivation. It certainly did with Dad.

But Dad was good with animals. Really good. That could not be denied. He would show a care and patience with horses and cows that was uncommon amongst his peers, where it was much more usual to use a stick than a carrot. He would happily spend huge amounts of time coaxing a timid horse into its training or working with various cattle.

He did genuinely seem to enjoy that work. But even his compassionate approach begot a downside, as it meant that Dad would over-commit his time to one animal, spend too long tending to it, at the expense of other jobs that might have been more pressing or more profitable in nature. And ultimately, it doesn't matter how much you might enjoy one particular element of something – having a vocation thrust upon you is never going to make for the most fulfilling career in the world.

I actually think he had a creative streak within him. In another life, he might have been an artist. Given a different set of circumstances he might have found fulfilment in exploring that side of himself, because he was definitely a thinker.

He used to write little bits of poetry. He carried around a copybook where he would jot down pieces of this and that, messy scribbles he composed between the faded blue lines.

Recently, my sister came to me with one of those notebooks

and we found the following poem, which Dad had written at some point during our childhood.

> *Perhaps there is a heaven.*
> *Perhaps we're in it now.*
> *And all the things that happened were meant to be somehow,*
> *Do you think it was all crafted by some outstanding feat?*
> *By angels, gods and spirits,*
> *Just so we could meet!*
> *Life is so exciting when you just sit back*
> *And trust! Let God take care of all the things*
> *You think, you must!*
> *There are things he may have sent our way,*
> *Things we may have missed!*
> *Things we could enjoy or need but instead we just resist!*

I love that poem, and it's a good example of the bits and pieces he used to do. He'd always do some, tipping away at it now and then, but there was rarely any prolonged period of attention devoted towards it, and you never got the feeling that he did enough. It felt like there might have been a deep well of possibilities within him, but he only ever jotted down the overspill. He never sank the line to see how much he could find.

Who knows what might have happened if he had?

He was like that, though. He'd have flurries of productivity followed by long periods of apathy, where the curtains would come down and all light in him would vanish for a while.

From my vantage point it seems obvious now that he must

have had some form of depression. But back then, in rural Ireland, we were still a long way off from having the vocabulary to identify it as such. Back then he was only lazy, inconsistent and lacking in commitment. We would never have looked at him and wondered if it was possible that his problems were anything other than a basic fault in his character.

It was under this cloud that the farm and the family finances began to creak. The farm rarely generated enough money to turn a profit. Often it would need to be subsidised out of what Mammy brought home from her job. These burdens became so heavy that it was eventually decided that Dad would have to take up a second job alongside the farm work in the hopes of keeping the nine of us and our farm afloat.

He began with a massage course. Why that and why then? I couldn't say. But training to be a masseur was the first possible second career I remember. And it didn't pan out. He never really got to a position where he could get it off the ground as a business or make money from it.

There were other courses too; lots of them. He was forever finding a new interest, diving headlong into it, then dropping it just as suddenly in favour of flitting off to something else.

Whether he repeated this cycle because he soon discovered that massage, or any of the potential careers that followed it, were bad ideas, or whether it was because he'd never really committed to any of them in the first place, I don't know. Perhaps it was a yearning for something new, anything new, and a change from the monotony of country living and a litter of kids. An attempt to make something of himself, or a reprieve from a marriage and a situation he didn't know how to navigate, before telling himself he was just being silly and it was all nonsense and trying something else. Perhaps it was all of that. But I was young and all I could see was a man repeatedly changing.

The thing that stuck the longest was a gig as a travelling salesman whereby he would tour the country selling life assurance. It meant that he would have to be out on the road a lot, gone for large chunks of time, leaving Mammy alone with seven of us kids, the farm and her own full-time job.

I'm not sure why this was thought to be a good idea at the time. Maybe it was because it was easy to access, requiring little training and hence shortening the risk of Dad moving on again before any money came in. Maybe it was decided that since it wasn't a rigid nine-to-five, it would leave spare time for Dad to work the farm when he wasn't on the road, although he hadn't exactly demonstrated himself to be capable of that sort of workload previously.

Partly, and this is pure conjecture on my part, I think it was because it got him away and gave both Mammy and himself some space from each other, which must have initially seemed like a blessed relief for both of them.

If the hope was that this forced absence would breed a renewed sense of fondness between them, unfortunately it was a failed venture, because it quickly became apparent that Dad relished the freedom the road gave him for a different reason.

This new lifestyle provided him with the out that he'd never quite had the wherewithal to seek himself while surrounded by all of us. It got him away from the farm, it got him away from his family, it got him away from all these responsibilities he'd had weighing around him since he was nineteen and gave him a peek at the single life he'd failed to have as a youth.

As it turned out, it was an experience he found liberating.

The times when he was home, he was almost a ghost. He'd sleep late into the mornings – again – and would often be gone by the evenings when we were home from school. We were seeing less of him now that we'd ever done before.

We began to notice the fights. They'd happen when we were abed. Mammy was never one to shout, so they'd be conducted through whispered voices, still barely restrained through the hurt, in a failed effort not to wake us. Mammy was being abandoned and Dad didn't seem to have it in him to care.

It happened slowly and more quietly than you might have imagined, but they drifted away from each other. Over time, the whispered arguments ceased, and a silence took their place, which in many ways was far worse.

Looking back on it now, it seems obvious that Dad had checked out of the relationship long before the marriage ever actually ended. He didn't appear to be interested in doing anything to fix it or to amend his behaviour. From Mammy's point of view, lumped as she was with the mantle of breadwinner, primary caregiver and full-time bad guy, I don't know how she would have even had the energy left over to try and elicit a change in a man who was really only treading water in a situation he didn't have the energy to either leave or repair. All the while, the road became ever more attractive to him.

This is only my imagination, but I do fancy that during those times he had on the road he indulged himself in this fantasy of being a single man, hiding the fact that he had a family, representing himself as a man unencumbered by anything except the day and the job and the person in front of him. I picture him introducing himself to strangers as Justin Brady from Roscommon, the only true things he'd admit to, before spinning them a yarn about the lives he had never succeeded in leading, living out for a night the futures he could have had.

The obvious assumption is that this would lead him towards infidelities, and there is one of those of which I am absolutely sure. I can only presume that there were many more.

The one I know about for certain I learned of via a message that came through to his phone when I was sixteen or seventeen. I happened to read it, not through any sense of suspicion or act of maliciousness on my part, but because the phone happened to be beside me at the time, and it only seemed natural to have a look in case it might be important, something that Dad would need to know immediately, for work.

The message I read was very obviously not from a work colleague. It was far too familiar for that. Reading it was the sort of thing that makes you feel cold in your stomach, but I didn't react right away. I kept that information to myself for some time.

When I finally broached the subject with Mammy, we talked it out and she indicated that she was aware of it but didn't know what to do. They had seven kids and a farm together. She was in uncharted territory, and the common social action at the time would have been to do very little. Have it out internally, a private dispute between spousal partners maybe, but nothing more drastic would have been considered an appropriate form of action in Bellanagare or Elphin or in much of anywhere in the Ireland of that time.

Divorce had become legal in Ireland during the mid-nineties, but it was still seen as a nuclear option by many people, something that was unthinkably destructive and perhaps best left unused, which was sort of how my folks viewed it too.

Within the Brady family, a number of different methods for dealing with a broken relationship had already been trialled by my grandparents on the Brady side, back when they were much younger and still raising their own children.

Granny and Grandad Brady came from the Catholic generation where marriage was more like Ronseal – it did exactly what it said on the tin, meaning that you stayed married until either one or the both of you were dead. So, when they too drifted apart in the outwardly silent but inwardly chaotic style that was the fashion of the time, all that happened was that Granny Brady moved out with the younger children to her mother's homeplace near Tulsk, and Grandad Brady stayed in the farmhouse in Corrigeen.

They never separated. They just happened to live in

different villages now but were still married. They never spoke about it. It was just the way things were. Grandad was never a talker, and the idea that he might ever discuss this sort of thing was so ridiculous that you would have had a better chance of getting blood from a rock than of getting a word out of him about it.

One consequence was that, from then on, Grandad Brady only ever referred to his wife as 'that woman', and never in the glowing terms of a once-affectionate or lovelorn partner. Granny, for her part, took great pride in the fact that she continued to honour her marriage vows, long after she had moved away from her husband and ceased any pretence of having a life together.

In all seriousness, it wasn't a clean separation for either them or their family.

There was a tug-of-war over the children; half went with Granny and half stayed with Grandad. Sometimes Grandad would collect the children from school without telling Granny, who would turn up ten minutes later, none the wiser. It can't have been easy on Dad or any of his siblings.

This all happened long before we were ever around. By the time we were growing up, it was only natural to us that Grandad and Granny Brady should live separately. That's the way it was and, we assumed, the way it had always been. That our other grandparents, Grandad and Nanny Dowd, still lived together in apparent harmony, didn't cause us a second's pause. We never linked together the evidence that one situation might be odd when compared to the other.

So, no; divorce wasn't really considered a serious option for my parents when this was the history that came before them.

However, even with that ruled out, I became an advocate for her (and us) moving out. I backed the idea that Mammy should pack us up and leave the farmhouse behind. Yes, it would be shit for everyone involved. Yes, it would be especially hard on my younger brothers and sisters. There would be no escaping that. But as things stood they were worse.

Even before the marriage began to break down, Mammy had never had an easy time of it in the farmhouse.

Granny Brady, unwilling to speak to her husband, would still call to the farm regularly to bless this, or throw holy water over that, or to press miraculous medals into our hands and try and make us say our prayers.

Granny Brady also held some sort of strange dominion over the front room of the house, the 'good room' as many people will know it; that place at the front of the house designed to never, ever be used, save on the rare occasion that a dignitary of high standing, like the priest, would come to call, and where we held the stations of the cross.

Our brood had grown too big to allow such an extravagance, so the 'good room' had turned into our play room, with a computer and a box of toys plonked amidst the iron-crisp doilies and pledge-cleaned cabinets. Granny referred to the computer as 'the devil's box'. She would frequently lambaste Mammy for having taken over 'her room', and would complain at length about the presence of 'the devil's box' in there, which was Mammy's fault too.

On at least one of the occasions when Dad had taken to his bed, I remember Granny following Mammy around the house, shouting things at her like: 'You dragged him down. You did it. You dragged him down.'

It was barely surprising that Dad's problems hadn't gone unnoticed by either of his parents, but while Grandad chose to berate his son, Granny had decided that Mammy was to blame, which was, quite frankly, unbelievable. I honestly don't know whether, in their dark and quiet moments, either of them ever considered that they may have been to blame.

The only real question here is how on earth Mammy ever stood it for so long. She endured a colossal level of abuse. She was a hero, and yet for so long she was only ever the killjoy bad guy in our eyes, always cracking the whip and assigning jobs.

I feel guilty for misunderstanding things so badly.

Mammy did make the move, eventually. She got lucky when a house became available in Toberrory, beside her parents, Grandad and Nanny Dowd. It would mean that we'd all still be in the same area, close to the farm in Corrigeen, close to the disco in Bellanagare, close to the schools in Mantua, close to football in Elphin, which allowed some semblance of a routine to continue for the younger members of the family especially, but away from Dad.

I felt bad about pushing the move because, at seventeen, I thought I was at least old enough to pretend that I might be an adult, and I'd had a long time to fully appreciate what a toxic mess my parents' relationship had become. But, at the same time, how well can anyone truly understand the private relationship between two other people? What chance did my younger brothers and sisters have, the youngest of whom was only eleven? They were only babies, and while they couldn't have thought things were fine, they certainly couldn't appreciate how bad they really were. To them, it was just a catastrophe that didn't seem to come from anywhere. My brother Donal, especially, just couldn't understand where on earth Dad would go, which, in fairness, was a good question.

The answer to that was depressingly similar to what had happened to Grandad and Granny Brady before; Mammy moved to Toberrory, taking us with her, and Dad stayed with the farm and the farmhouse. We squeezed into a smaller house, older children sharing rooms with younger, which I thought was a major sacrifice for a teenager of such advanced seniority as I was then, and Dad was left alone with the livestock, since Grandad had by this time moved into a care home.

This is the point from which things properly started to deteriorate for Dad. This was true for the farm and it was true for himself too. How much looking after him we as a family, and Mammy in particular, had done became evident once he was left to fend for himself. Very quickly, various elements of basic habitual upkeep slipped away.

Being on the road a lot, staying in hotels and eating out, gave Dad a false illusion of self-care. He didn't have to worry about washing bed sheets or buying groceries or any of the myriad of little jobs that go into keeping a home liveable on a daily basis.

The farmhouse was the first thing to suffer. The indifference that had come to characterise his attitude towards the farm was turned towards the farmhouse as well. Whenever we might call over, we'd always notice some new sign of decline: the fire was never lit, the turf had run out, the heating wasn't working, all of which conspired to give damp a foothold within the premises.

Damp wasn't the only thing to take hold. A lonely stillness had invaded the space between the walls that had once been our home. It was a permanent resident now. It didn't shift, not even when we came to call.

The farmhouse was a sad place to be in; a home that had once been full of energy and life was now just a house with no warmth, no food and no comfort. So, what happened was that Dad started calling down to the new house, to Mammy's house. It was probably this mixture of isolation, neglect and a genuine want to see us that spurred him to do it, but what it created was a weird situation for everyone.

He'd never call ahead or ask permission from Mammy, he would simply stroll in the door and begin doing things like he would if he were at his own home back in Corrigeen; he'd make a cup of tea, or pick morsels from a pot of stew that would be set on the oven. They were always little actions, almost too small to make an issue of, but the familiarity with which he did them made it seem like he was either refusing to acknowledge the purpose of Mammy's action, or simply ignoring her wishes outright.

As kids we didn't really know what to do. Mammy had

made it very clear that he was more than welcome to spend time with us, but if he wanted to do that then he should collect us and bring us up to the farmhouse. She'd left that place to get away from him, and it was there, all set up for him. He could have us any time he liked, but he should respect her wishes and do it over there.

We were caught in this middle ground whereby we didn't want to betray Mammy, but we also didn't want to ignore Dad. He was being unfair, even the younger siblings understood that. He was not respecting the perfectly reasonable boundaries that Mammy was trying to maintain. The conundrum was that we were still delighted to see him. He was our dad. We loved him and we were sad for him. He already seemed so lost.

We couldn't decide whether we should engage with him when he called down, which would have been disloyal towards Mammy, or if we should refuse to interact with him, which seemed like a brutally cruel thing for us to do. It was an impossible situation. No matter what way we moved, we would end up hurting one of our parents. And at the time it was hard not to see this as a situation of Dad's own making.

His unannounced visits to the new house in Toberrory continued until it got to the stage where Mammy started retreating to her room every time he appeared. At that stage, we couldn't sit on the fence any longer. We began to say to him that we were happy to spend time with him, but that we should do it up in the farmhouse. Going with him was no problem to us. He just needed to give us some notice and that's exactly what we'd do. Mammy's boundaries would be respected, we'd get time with our dad, and he wouldn't be so lonely.

At these suggestions Dad would generally make some vague agreement. *Yeah. Sure. Maybe next time.* But it would never materialise.

Partly, this was because he'd have had to set the house to rights. He would have had to get some food in, turn on the heating, and so on. And I just don't think he possessed the ability to pull that off.

Slowly, he stopped dropping down to us at all.

He fell deeper and deeper into a malaise. On the odd occasions when we did call up to the farmhouse, it didn't seem like there was anyone living there. The cold of the house would be rivalled only by the thick smell of damp. There was also unopened mail piled up beside the front door, letters from creditors amassing like an angry mob.

This was another, even more alarming side of his decline. His profligacy with money had been apparent even when we all lived together. Now, it began to spiral out of all control.

It's very easy to owe money when you run a farm. It's how the system is built since so much of a farm's cash flow is seasonal in nature. For crops, you're not going to get paid until you've harvested and sold them. It's similar with livestock, you don't get paid until you've gotten them fat and ready.

In order to do that, you need lots of feed, fertiliser, diesel for vehicles, maybe a vet visit and things like that. Many of the industries that have been built up around supplying farmers with the things they need on a daily basis have established a system of accounts, like a tab, that runs for each farm and farmer. You take what feed you need, they note it down, and at the end of the season you settle your bill.

Dad had been taking the feed from the local supplier, but he had not been settling the bill. Where had the money gone? Most likely it would have been because he hadn't done the work required on the farm, so he hadn't generated enough income to turn a profit or break even, which then allowed the bills to pile up.

Something similar happened when he tried to develop the farm. He'd borrowed money to build new sheds, which got sort of built. Then, when the fields he rented to keep his livestock on came up for sale, he borrowed money against the value of the farmhouse to buy them. The money came in, and the money went out, but the fields were never bought.

The worst of the lot was when he took out a car loan in my mother's name and then failed to pay that off. That turned into a whole nasty situation that took a long time to rectify.

It wasn't that he was a nefarious financial fraudster, although all of those loan situations were pretty awful. It was that he struggled to complete the things he began. He'd start a process, get things moving, but then fail to organise himself properly to deal with the continuing demands of that process. As the deadlines and the missed payments mounted up, instead of being proactive and trying to negotiate or even just asking for help from the people around him, he would allow things to escalate to a level where it was all too much for him, at which stage he would simply disengage, shut down and cease to communicate.

This cycle of behaviour had been firmly established before we ever left the farmhouse, and as kids we'd even been trained into playing a role in aiding and abetting it, to a certain extent at least.

People, most likely creditors, would ring looking for Dad. He'd normally be in bed and, as kids, our first instinct was to say what was honest, so we'd tell whoever was calling that Dad was in bed. This was unacceptable, so bed quickly became the 'office'. When people rang, we were to say that he was in the 'office'. But as the calls got angrier the 'office' became 'away out at work'. He was 'away out at work', leave a message and we'll get him to ring you back.

Of course, Dad would rarely ring any of them back.

Occasionally people, again most likely creditors, would show up at the farmhouse in person and demand to see Dad. Those conversations would generally be taken outside. How they progressed, I can only guess, but you'd imagine that some threats were delivered by the creditor and some stalling was done by Dad.

He'd get in over his head like this repeatedly. And it was usually the same cause. It was because he'd made the promises, he'd tied himself and his money to the commitments, but then he hadn't followed through and done the work. He'd lost interest or disengaged and the only answer he could find was either to try and sleep it off, or to hit the road and see if he could run away.

Many other farmers in Ireland have similar financial struggles, similar problems with isolation and mental health. Men of rural Ireland are not allowed to fail. They are supposed to know what to do. They are supposed to be islands of solidity and strength. They are supposed to be *men*, in the way that *men* supposedly used to be. Which is a fiction, a skewed perception that serves only to pin these men in their place, making them ashamed to ask for help, embarrassed that they haven't been able to get their affairs in order by themselves. It's a trap that is so hard for people to break out of. And many don't.

At the farmhouse, the electricity became intermittent since he hadn't been paying that bill either. You'd drop up and you'd never know if he was going to be there or not. The house never looked lived in, and he had taken to vanishing for chunks of time that got longer and longer with each subsequent disappearance.

He wouldn't answer his phone, often it wouldn't ring at all, so we took to asking the neighbours if they'd seen his car.

A few days ago, maybe, they'd reply. But not in a while.

Those periods of vacancy grew from days to weeks to months until he just wasn't around at all. Occasionally he might turn up at something. He might have missed four or five Brady family gatherings in a row, but then he'd appear. We grew not to expect to see him, so it would always be a surprise, like, 'Oh, you're here.'

You'd chat. You'd try to ask him where he'd been and what he'd been doing; not accusingly, not from any desperate sense of curiosity, but just for want of something to say. It didn't matter what you asked him though, because he'd never give you a straight answer.

Ah, this and that, he'd say. Here and there.

He'd take pride in not giving any information away, like he was being cute through his avoidance. But it meant that, since we could never get anything meaningful from doing it, we just stopped asking him things altogether. What was the point?

When we saw him, we were civil, but there wasn't any avenue for a relationship beyond that because he wouldn't communicate on that level. He had withdrawn from us completely. Over time, Dad drifted so far away that he became nothing more than a stranger called Justin. Which is what we started calling him.

Justin, the man who used to be our dad.

Everyone in the locality knew about this. How could they not? News travels fast along the hedgerows, so we never bothered trying to hide it. Sometimes a neighbour would ask us how Justin was. We'd reply honestly: 'I haven't seen him in six months, I haven't a notion how he is.' It became normal.

Sometimes we'd get reports, from friends and the like, that he'd been spotted at an auction in Tipperary, or at a mart in Cork, odd places where it didn't seem like he had any business being. He wouldn't have been farming at this stage. Why was he at the marts?

The cattle had been sold in batches as Justin had needed the money, leaving only horses on the land. True to form, he wasn't the best keeper of these horses either. They were frequently untended, would get thin and would break out of their fields from boredom and from a need for food.

The general consensus among the community was that this was our problem as a family. It didn't matter that Justin was the one who owned them or that Justin was the one neglecting things. We were still his sons and daughters, Mammy was still his wife, and so we were expected to deal with them when things got too bad to ignore.

Our reluctance to do this stemmed from the fact that if you showed any bit of interest in Justin's problems at all, all of a sudden they became your problems too, like you were guilty by association, which meant that whenever he disappeared, you became the one who was expected to sort things out.

My uncle Marty took up a lot of the slack here, because the horses were living animals after all, and they didn't deserve to be ignored. There was also the possibility that if the horses broke out, they might eventually make it as far as a main road, which could cause serious or fatal injury to themselves or to someone else.

So, Marty played a blinder, selflessly taking on a burden that he was under no obligation to shoulder.

As Justin became unmoored from us, he also became distrustful of society in general. In the United States there is a term for conspiracy theorists who believe that the entire apparatus of the state is actively conspiring to subdue and subjugate the masses. They're called deep-staters, and they believe that you should trust in nothing.

Justin became an Irish version of a deep-stater. On the rare times that he did talk, he would talk about the corruption within the gardaí, how they were turning the country into a police state, about the fraudulent and unlawful burdens they placed upon citizens of the country, like car insurance, and other things of that nature. He didn't rave or tear at his hair. He didn't scream and shout. He talked about these topics in relative calm. They were only facts, and he was only relaying them.

Justin had a jeep that he lived in, sleeping in the back whenever he didn't have another place to go. But this jeep was uninsured, untaxed and not officially roadworthy by legal Irish standards. When he wasn't using it, he'd park it up in out-of-the-way spots close to train stations or bus stations, vanishing to other parts of the country for weeks at a time, but intending to return to it whenever it was that he would need it again.

Because it was completely devoid of its legally required notices – no tax disc, no insurance disc – from time to time the jeep would get impounded, being mistaken for an abandoned vehicle, which is exactly what it would have looked like.

One time I got a call from a guard in Castlerea who turned out to be an old schoolfriend of my father's. It's pretty scary to get a phone call from the gardaí. Your mind has a million thoughts at once, none of which is, 'This is going to be a pleasant call.'

We've found your father's jeep, he said. We found it abandoned so we had to take it in. We didn't know it was his because it's registered to someone else, but it had all his stuff in the back. There's a sleeping bag, a washbag, clothes and papers. There's even a saddle and some other bits too.

I listened to all this and couldn't help but feel so sad to discover how he was living now.

You'll need to collect it, the guard continued. He'll probably need his stuff again, but the jeep won't be coming back. It's been here three weeks and the fines are worth more than the jeep. The jeep will be destroyed. But come collect his stuff and you can give it to him whenever he next turns up.

I said I would. We made our goodbyes and I hung up the phone.

The guard was only being nice. He knew the fines would never be paid. He was simply concerned for an old friend and a member of the local community who had lost his way. That he cared enough to call me at all really touched me.

It was all so sad, but it was a sadness tinged with embarrassment too. This was our father. This was who he was. This was how he acted. He did try to be discreet about it. He had taken himself away at least, but this didn't change the fact that it wasn't a healthy way of living, it wasn't a secret to anyone, and it wasn't the way any of us would have wanted it.

We loved our dad. He had been such a magically fun and entertaining presence in our lives when we were younger. But, that was half the problem. When he was around and engaged, he was fun, but I don't think he was ever a parent. That was left to Mammy, who had to earn a living and do the roles of two parents while he got lost within himself.

You'd get angry with him for it all as well. What was wrong

with him? There was a house there for him. All he needed to do was show up, reconnect the heating and reconnect the electricity and he could live in his own way, but he could do it near us.

When we did see him, it was hard not to sense a pride emanating from him for having gone this far, for having taken himself so firmly off the grid, for having successfully managed to fall between the cracks and evade the attention of whoever was supposed to be watching him; be that the state, or us, or his own demons chasing him from the past lives he'd lived.

And then he died. And that was the end of all of that.

It happened when I was abroad. It shouldn't have come as such a shock, he'd so obviously fallen so far from anything that could be termed as healthy, but it did. Death is always a shock, and after all, Justin was only fifty. It didn't matter that he'd slowly turned into a faintly sighted ghost over the last ten years of his life. He was my dad. I couldn't believe that he was really dead.

I'd been out on a six-week performance gig in the summer of 2017 for the Islamic Games in Azerbaijan. We'd just done the closing ceremony and were having a wrap party when Michelle rang me. Mammy had been trying to get through to me for hours, but my network reception was faulty, so Michelle had eventually gotten me on a web call instead.

I was glad it was her who told me. I don't know why, but I was glad Mammy hadn't gotten through first.

The only person that I really knew in Azerbaijan was Aisling, my performing partner. Everyone else was practically a stranger. I'd gone out into the hallway to take the call, one finger squeezed into my ear to block out the music from the party. I could barely hear what was being said to me.

When I finally understood, I sank to the floor and began balling my eyes out, not fully believing it was true, trying desperately to think of the last time I had seen him, the last things we'd said, how he had seemed, if I should have noticed anything.

I didn't know what had happened to him, and I didn't know what to do next. I didn't know how I was going to get home. I didn't want to walk back into the party and announce that my dad was dead, so I just stayed where I was, curled into the steps of a stairwell in a country that felt light-years away from my home.

I was eventually found by Aisling when it took so long for me to return to the party. She discovered me on the stairs, and herself and the festival organisers immediately swung into action. They were amazing, taking me back to my accommodation and helping me get sorted on the first flight back to Ireland.

I wasn't the only one abroad, so it took a little time for the family to assemble before we could bury him, which we did in Elphin in June 2017.

Later, I found out what happened to him.

Prior to his death, Justin had been at my uncle Robert's house and had been complaining about a pain in his leg. It hadn't seemed overly serious, but it had been enough for him to comment on it, which was unusual for him. Justin had left there and gone back down to Cork, where he was in a relationship, but none of us knew to what level or for how long.

While he was in Cork the pain in his leg had persisted, enough so that Justin finally decided to go and get it checked out. However, at this stage he no longer believed in conventional medicine, and was instead interested in holistic treatments, healers and alternative therapies. The healer he went to told him to light a candle and go to sleep. In three days, the healer assured him, the pain would have passed.

Justin did this. He lit his candle and climbed into bed.

He was found dead on the floor of his bedroom. He'd had a clot in his leg and this was what had been causing the pain. It had dislodged and moved to his heart, which had caused him to go into arrest, killing him.

We were sad about this, but we were angry also. Healers and lighting candles? What did he expect? It was a horrible concoction of grief and fury. And worst of all was that there was no real way to square with it.

It had happened. End of story. Full stop. Good luck and thanks.

And then life went on, as it always does, cruelly indifferent.

It wasn't until a year later that I got a full jolt of realisation that the old man was really dead. I was rarely back in Elphin. Mammy lived in the house in Toberrory, while I was living in Athlone and working all over. I never had any cause to visit Corrigeen or the pasts that it contained, until one day on my way to Letterkenny I realised that I would be driving close by so I went to stop by the grave. Once there, I got a smack of reality.

He was really gone.

You see, we didn't miss him in the way you might expect a family to miss a parent. He had been gone for so much of our lives already, that in a way it was hard to believe he wasn't still out there somewhere, wandering the back roads of the country or sleeping in his jeep, a vague and undefined presence in the shadows of your mind, but an active and moving being all the same.

That makes you feel terrible. You're sad that they're gone, but you're embarrassed too that, more often than not, you don't even remember that they *are* gone. One of my uncles also died recently – Robert, the man who had put me on top of Cleo that day in our front field. While fencing close to a riverbank, he had fallen in and drowned.

At first, no one knew what had happened to him and a search took place for a few days. This concluded when his body was found a kilometre downriver from where he had been fencing. I was in Abu Dhabi at the time visiting my brother, Gerard.

That death was felt more keenly by me for the basic reason that Robert was around more. Robert left a gap when he died. Justin didn't do that because, in so many ways, he was gone already.

It made me think about all the stupid shit people do. All the second-guessing that happens, trying to divine what it is that other people are thinking. All that wasted effort, born from the fact that we rarely try to honestly communicate with each other about what is actually going on. All those relationships that break down for no other reason than people didn't know how to properly talk to one another.

With Justin, things went that way, getting progressively worse, snowballing out of control until it ended, abruptly and without fanfare, on the floor of a bedroom in Cork. So much unnecessary pain, confusion and question marks around my father for me, my siblings, and even my mother.

I've guessed at a lot of reasons why I think my parents' relationship dissolved, but I don't really know the why of it, and I'm not sure that Mammy does either. How could she when she was faced with a man who would barely talk? And none of us can go and ask him now. We can't have that discussion anymore. We can only surmise as to why he felt the need to disengage from us as a family and recreate himself into this nomadic, single-man lifestyle.

We don't even know if he ended up happy in that new place he made for himself. I hope so. But I don't know that, and I never will.

I do know that in the last twelve months of his life he had started to reconnect with his kids and reach out more. At the funeral, the family started to share stories of how he had shown up, visited and called each one of us at some point in the recent past. He'd even stopped in randomly on Mammy. They'd had tea and a lovely chat and he'd gone again, just like it was a normal visit.

For me, he rang one day asking if I was in Athlone. I was,

and he said that he was at the train station with a couple of hours to burn. I met him for some food and coffee. It was one of those strange chats where we avoided all the big stuff and just chatted about work, weather, the state of the nation, and so on. I'm glad it happened. I took a photo with him and sent it to the family WhatsApp group with the comment, 'Look who it is.' It was nice. I cherish that memory now.

He did have that other relationship with this lady in Cork. She was at the funeral and she was welcomed into the proceedings. Why not? But we don't know her so well, so I don't know if she thought he was happy.

Maybe one of these days I'll go and I'll ask her.

There's a part of Justin's character that makes me worry for myself a little bit. I have had a number of passions in my life, things that have taken up centre stage in how I perceive myself and how I seek to organise my future, football and circus being the two obvious examples. But when I was done with football, I was done. I didn't really agonise too much over leaving it behind and I haven't missed it since. This has happened too with teaching and with the FCA and with any number of other gadget and gizmo-orientated fads I have picked up, delved into and then left behind.

Dad did that, with his farm and his massage courses and his travelling salesman job, even his family. He picked it up, then lost interest and wandered off. I have the same nomadic tendencies.

Am I the same? Is this what I do as well, albeit in a different mode?

What if I get two or five or ten years into my circus career and then give up? What if I did that to one of my personal relationships? What if I did that to Michelle?

This thought terrifies me more than I can say.

Ultimately, I'm going to have to be grateful for the memories of him I do have and hope I can learn from them. Because, if I can't, then I'm screwed too.

None of this is meant to cast me as the victim. I'm not a victim. My bullying had victims. My anger had victims, of which I am not one. But it was a big part of the reasoning behind my actions, it is why I so often felt the need to vent and make others feel small.

I'm not proud of it. And lurking behind all the progress I've made over the last decade or so is the knowledge that there is a bully still within me, strong and waiting and ready. I retain the capacity to be a colossal dick, to retreat back to my old hiding places of 'only having the craic' but doing it at the expense of someone else.

It's a fear that I'm not sure I can shake. But it's a fear I don't think I want to shake either, because I don't ever want to forget.

TEN

HOMECOMING

(The economics of art, the culchies, the thicks
and the hopeful nature of self-discovery.)

It's a grey day in September 2019 and I am driving again, navigating the roads from Limerick to Athlone. My car is still a safe space; the hum of the tyres against the bitumen provides a steady undertone to the gentle roar of the engine. It's warm and comfortable, but I'm looking forward to getting back to Michelle, back to our home and the life we share.

Michelle and I have been together through thick and thin over the past fourteen years; through successes and failures. We met each other when we were seventeen and have managed to make it through going to school in different counties, attending college on different sides of the country, and then working for large periods of time in different parts of the world.

We have both always been pretty independent as people, but, within our relationship as a couple, we still support each other. Michelle has been there for me through losses, deaths, wins and uncertainties. She was with me the day I decided that I could not go back teaching, that I needed to pursue this circus life instead. She encouraged me to do it and has backed me ever since.

In her life, she's been a more successful footballer than

I ever managed to be. She won an All-Ireland football title with Leitrim in 2007. She took me with her on the victory holiday with the team for that. I did the same for her when I won the Connacht title with Roscommon in 2010. We've shared so much together. But we've also missed lots of stuff too, more than can be listed. She has been the one who has found me crying at home because I've run out of paid circus work, or because I'm going to miss rent, or because I have had to borrow money again. She has always been there.

We are very different people from who we were when we met. We have grown together and changed together. I've been guilty of neglecting her at times, becoming super-focused and consumed in my work. My obsessive nature is something I'm still working on.

I don't know what I'd so without her.

She's the unsung hero of this story. She's been unsung on purpose. I wanted to keep our lives together mostly private. I've put her through so much with all this turmoil over the last few years, I didn't want me telling my story to be another part of that burden. She is her own person, with her own life and her own story. And what we have together is special, so I've tried to keep it that way. I hope you can understand. Our relationship is not perfect, of course; I'm not sure a perfect relationship exists. It's one that takes nurturing, as every relationship does. We try to lift each other up and be there for each other. We are figuring it out just like everyone else. I cannot thank her enough for all she has done for me. Words cannot do it justice.

I drive on, towards her. This has been a strange year. I've created a brand-new outdoor show with Aisling called *Sub Rosa*, toured one we had already made but re-worked called *How to Square a Circle* to great success, been involved in the creation of two other shows with other companies, performed another Vicar Street run of *Riot*, and now I'm writing this book. If I'm honest, between the deaths of Justin and Robert and all the life work in between, it's been a strange few years. I'm still struggling with lots of competing things in my life and it's beginning to dawn on me that this might always be the way.

I'm far down this arts path now: I've done three years on *Riot*, I have been successful in securing grant funding from the Arts Council, with Aisling I've begun to make my own work, but the lack of financial reward and the complete absence of stability is still a concern. Alongside that is the expanding belief that I think – no, I *know* – that I'd like to have a family. I know too that it's only with Michelle that I'd ever want to do that. But I don't know how I'd balance the infrequency and uncertainty of my arts career against the needs of being the parent I'd want to be.

I don't particularly want to return to teaching, but I know I could. I know that I'd be good at it, and I know it would fully address all those concerns.

And yet there's what happened in Roscommon just this last summer of 2019. Oh, sweet Roscommon. Since then the earth beneath my feet has shifted again, and the only familiar and consistent thing is my uncertainty.

In the face of all else, that remains undimmed.

However, before I talk about that, I need to go back two years, to the spring of 2017 and the birth of *How to Square a Circle*, the show that should never have been.

Aisling Ní Cheallaigh was and is my circus partner. We'd gotten to know each other beneath the Fidget Feet umbrella, working for the awesome artistic parentage of Chantal McCormick and Jym Daly. During that time, Aisling had been struck by an idea for a show.

Like the more traditional circuses before it, Fidget Feet is more of a family than a company, but this one was a collection of unrelated people brought together by a common desire to fly and nurtured through Fidget Feet's innate ability to provide opportunity and guidance for young artists.

Within that family, during rehearsals or performances of Fidget Feet shows, while crammed into cramped changing rooms or tiny canteens, this collection of people would almost inevitably begin to share and expand on whatever personal problems were currently challenging them.

Now, sometimes the need for this therapy was caused *by* Fidget Feet because of the maniacally restrained budgets and frantically packed performance calendars they operate within.

Cheaper than Therapy was the show idea that Aisling originally had, an ensemble performance about a group of disparate people coming together to share and grow. It was a good idea, and she brought it to Chantal, otherwise known as Mama Fidget, to get her thoughts.

Chantal agreed. It *was* a good idea. But it was a big idea, full of performers, crew and moving parts, and since Aisling had never made her own work before, aside from short solo acts, Chantal said she should simplify, start with something challenging but achievable. Aisling already had a performing relationship with me, so why didn't she devise a show that took advantage of that?

Aisling took this advice on board and approached me with a new idea.

Since I began my circus journey, Aisling has been my greatest champion. She's been the one to big me up when my confidence was low, and to talk me up to anyone else who would listen. There's no way I'd still be in this game if it weren't for her dedication, nurturing and care.

We work well together. She's really good for getting things moving with ideas and actions, which counterbalances my tendency to be only useful once I'm in the room. In turn, I provide a grounding for Aisling, giving her a solid base as a circus performer and artistic partner, someone to trust in and rely upon. A friend, in other words.

Her new idea had a conceptual foundation in mathematics, namely the impossibility of geometrically squaring a circle. The idea appealed because it struck her as being similar to the frustrating and often futile attempts that we as people make when trying to communicate ourselves and connect with one another. We try and we fail but we always try again. Added to that, and on a distinctly more simplistic level, two of our primary circus apparatuses were her aerial hoop and my cyr wheel, meaning there was a duplicity between form and function in the idea.

It was another good idea, good enough to maybe get some Arts Council funding behind it, and I was jazzed when I saw her proposal, but I quickly noticed that within her show outline there wasn't an awful lot of practical detail on what the show might actually look like once it was put onto a stage, and I felt I could see exactly that.

I took her proposal and redrafted it based on the images I could see so clearly in my head. In typical artistic fashion, we had left this work until the last possible moment, so as the Arts Council deadline loomed, I spent the night before channelling my inner-Kerouac, surrounded by tea and biscuits, riffing away on the concepts that Aisling had laid down.

What I sent back to her was also good. Aisling agreed. It *was* definitely good, yet she couldn't help but notice that what I had written was, once again, an entirely different show from what she'd first proposed. Cocooned safely within my own smugness I insisted that while this was certainly true, it was because my idea was better.

Somehow, Aisling resisted the temptation to skewer me, and we spent the rest of the night, right up until the deadline the next day, figuring out a compromise that blended Aisling's theoretical concept with my practical outline.

This hashed-together version of both our ideas was submitted in a haze of caffeine and last-minute digital scrambling, leaving us frazzled and with a strange feeling of incompleteness since we now had months to wait before a decision was made.

The months passed slowly until, one day, a letter arrived. Our application had been successful. We'd been granted thirty grand to make our show.

When I first heard the amount of money that was now ours, my eyes widened, and my imagination went into overdrive. I was foreseeing the capacity to have laser lights, flying walls and space landings in this show if we wanted to, because this was a stack of cash hitherto unimaginable in my concept of the arts world. I mean, thirty grand! What opulence.

This delirium evaporated rather quickly when we sat down to confirm the provisional budget we'd originally submitted. It's scary how quickly costs can mount up. There's rehearsal space rental, costume purchase and design, prop purchase and design, rigging purchase and design, lighting purchase and design, sound design, crew fees, mentor fees, travel, accommodation, food, marketing, posters, flyers, online advertising, insurance and contingency. This was supposed to be a two-person piece, but it was going to take the employment of nine other people to create, produce and perform this show.

The money vanished before our eyes, disappearing between the lines of our spreadsheet and leaving us in a place whereby we were rapidly coming to understand our new reality; namely, that we were going to spend a number of months pouring every inch of our souls into making this proposal a reality, devoting ourselves entirely to it, and might only end up getting paid somewhere around three grand for our hundreds of hours of work and toil. Perhaps the days of Michelle finding me crying in the shower about my lack of earning power were not over after all.

There would be no laser lights. There would barely even be a pay day. I would not be coming out of this rich. I would not even be breaking even on my time commitment because of the worldwide phenomenon that always relegates artistic output below every other conceivable element of production. Techies and crew and bills all get paid; it's always the artist that takes the cut.

I'd seen this before in working with Fidget Feet, whereby Mama and Papa Fidget would regularly slash their own wages and charge for only a fraction of the time they'd put into a gig just to allow it to happen. I'd sworn to myself I would do things differently should I ever be in that position. But this wasn't going to happen. It's an insoluble conundrum, born out of a lack of resources available for the art form, and I'd fallen foul of it just like most of the other Irish circus folk before me had.

This highlighted the double-edged-sword nature of the funding we'd been granted. In many ways it felt like an official validation of us as artists in our own rights. It gave us a permission to create, not because you need the Arts Council's permission to do anything, far from it, but because we seemed like newborn babies in the artistic world, and the fact that the Arts Council thought we could do what we said we'd do was a boon.

The challenging side of this was that, all of a sudden, I

had been promoted from my place of passive commentary, my place within Fidget Feet or Thisispopbaby where I could safely describe how, given a chance, I would do things differently, without the burden of actually having to prove myself. I would have to start practising these things I was preaching.

The thirty grand award would allow us eight weeks spread out over six months to research, develop, create, rehearse and perform the show. This sounds like a lot, but it isn't. We had no clue how to bring our own ideas to life as a show that would make sense *and* be entertaining. We were foals on the prairie, fresh to the world, sticky and teetering as we tried to find our feet. Most of that time would be spent learning *how* to do this thing, which left us only a few weeks at the end to actually do it.

To compound this issue was the knowledge that while we could afford to bring more senior, experienced and accomplished artists in as mentors, like Chantal from Fidget Feet and the wonderful Lindsey Butcher of Gravity & Levity, we would only be able to do that for a number of days at a time, meaning that overall, we'd be working under our own guidance and direction.

It was a terrifying proposition, and it proved to be incredibly difficult.

We had a series of individual acts – wheel, hoop, doubles trapeze – that we were pretty certain we could incorporate into a cohesive whole, and we also had a good idea of the narrative that we wanted overarching all of this, but figuring out how all these pieces fit together while simultaneously expanding the narrative elements without the consistent presence of an eye external to us meant that a lot of our ideas didn't get as long as we'd have liked in order to mature.

The process pushed us both much further than we'd ever been pushed before, challenging us artistically, developing our understanding of the gap that exists between idea and execution, and personally, as we had to learn to work together in the most intensive circumstances we'd ever encountered while remaining collaboratively open and reliable.

This creation process was scheduled to culminate with two sets of performances: a premiere in Blanchardstown on the edge of Dublin, and a follow-up in Athlone, a homecoming of sorts for me, being adjacent to Roscommon and the place where I live with Michelle.

As we entered into the final week of production, a familiar doubt started to creep over us. It was similar to the one that had taken hold in the run-up to the premiere of *Riot* two years previously on the edges of leafy Merrion Square. Increasingly we were doubting whether or not what we were making was any good. A gap emerged between our hope and our expectation, because we expected it to be a disaster. As we got deeper into the week and closer to the premiere, we lost all sense of perspective regarding the quality of what we'd created, and the gap continued to widen.

This gap only gets closed when you perform and, assuming of course that things go even moderately well, you begin to feel the reaction of the crowd as a physical sensation that feeds your confidence and raises your capacity to perform.

Try as you might, it's not possible to give it full throttle during rehearsal while in front of empty seats. It means that there's always a part of the show that you cannot see until it's out there and you are living it. It's not that you don't give everything during rehearsals, you do. It's that rather there'll always be something missing that the presence of an audience will provide.

This loop finally got closed on a mid-week Wednesday in May in the Draiocht Theatre of Blanchardstown. It had been a blue-sky day at the start of summer, one of those where you actually notice that the light of day now spans the length of the evening. The show was attended by a mixture of family, friends and strangers. Among the crowd was Panti Bliss, who was joined by a number of other friends from the arts community with whom we had worked over the years, and it was these people more than any others who were cause for concern because, if we failed, they would be the first to know.

The crowd filed in, the lights went down and, over the course of the next hour, *How to Square a Circle* was born.

Afterwards, we scurried off stage to what we were pretty confident was enthusiastic applause and into the changing rooms where we got caught in the nerves of whether or not to go and face the familiar faces outside in the lobby. We were so far gone in our doubt that we weren't given to trust in the evidence of our senses. We dreaded the idea of being faced with politeness by our artistic peers. You know that your opposite number has not enjoyed your work when, forced into saying something, *anything* for the sake of politeness, they will reach for an obfuscation such as, 'Are you happy with how it went?' They want to say something without saying anything because they wish to spare your feelings. It's a death knell.

We did our best to reassure each other that things had gone well, and left the changing room.

Panti Bliss was one of the first people to approach me, loudly complaining about the cost of her taxi ride out to this venue so far removed from the city centre, which didn't sound to me like an encouraging start.

I've spent the worth of a week's wage getting out here, she declared with a twinkle glittering in her eyes.

Your wage or mine? I asked, duly playing my part.

Your wage, of course, she smiled.

Then she clapped me on the back, wrapped me in a hug and told me how much she'd liked it. Genuinely.

In my mind she said something benign like, *you did good, Ronan.* But that doesn't sound like something Panti would say. I don't really remember the words she said because the relief that she had enjoyed it had washed out any other detail.

Everyone else we talked to was similarly enthusiastic. Not once did we meet with muted politeness. The relief was sweet, and we progressed it on to another showing in Draiocht followed by two further performances in Athlone.

There it was. *How to Square a Circle* was alive. It had been terrifying, but it was a success.

We waited a little time for the dust to settle, allowing the taste of accomplishment to mature into a want for more. We'd done it, but that wasn't enough. After so much sweat and effort, it seemed like a waste not to try and give it a life beyond those fledgling performances. Certainly, my experience with *Riot* suggested that making a show was only the start. The thing only ever became really good when you started touring it. You needed the space to find the performance that only time and repetition could bring.

The Arts Council also had grants available for touring. If we could be successful in that, then *How to Square a Circle* would get a second lease of life, one that might even make a true homecoming to my county of Roscommon possible, which was something that appealed to me on a deep personal level.

Now, I know it's a strange one, but I felt a little weirded out by this concept of public funding for a tour. Why, I wondered, when we were already taking taxpayers' money to make the show, would we then go out and look for more money again to tour it, at which point we'd request a third payment by asking whoever turned up to see it for money?

Looking at it from the outside, it seemed to me like a con, a double and triple tax on people who may not have even asked for it. The capitalist in me is hard-line and says, if the show is any good, then it will sell the tickets and the ticket sales will pay for everything. Simple. No public funds required. If you can't find your audience and sell your tickets, then maybe the thing shouldn't exist in the first place.

But things aren't that simple, and capitalism is only a tool, albeit an excellent one, that should always be tempered by the greater social good. Working within the arts world, you begin to understand the stark realities of how little money there is available within this country to do anything of consequence.

For instance, as it currently stands, you might pay twenty euro (and in most cases, less) to see one of our shows. However, that twenty-euro price is not the true cost of the ticket as it is heavily subsidised by the Arts Council funding we receive. The true cost of that ticket, without the subsidy of Arts Council funding, would be much closer to one hundred euro per person if all costs were to be covered and a break-even position was to be achieved. Not a position of profit, break-even only. And that's still with us taking a hit and not charging for all the time we commit to training, rehearsing and performing in order to put the show out there.

Can you imagine trying to take a show around Ireland and having the stupidity to charge one hundred euro a ticket? People baulk at paying that sort of money for people like Bette Midler or Westlife – and rightly so. There's no chance an audience in Sligo or Cork or Roscommon are going to fork out that sum for people they don't know in an art form they're not familiar with. No venue in their right mind would take us either.

The stark reality is that, without the subsidy of public funds, performing arts of artistic merit would cease to even consider the notion of touring work at all, which is already something that far too few companies and artists attempt to do in the first place.

This high real-ticket cost isn't only peculiar to circus. Any performance above a one-hand theatre, dance or opera show would be similar. It just takes too many people and too much time to conduct the incredibly difficult task of creation. Art is hard, and it's expensive and it's vital. It's why it's always needed patronage of some sort, and that is true as far back in history as you'd care to look.

But circus contains overheads the other art forms do not. It costs a lot to get a performer up in the air, and it costs even more to keep them there safely. We work from that baseline of cost, like a hundred-metre sprinter starting twenty metres behind the blocks, before we have to consider all of the other things that the other art forms have as well.

And while you're chewing on that, chew on this. Funding of the arts in Ireland is amongst the worst in Europe. For a country that spends so much time banking off the fame of our writers, the reach of our musicians, or the depth of our cultural vibrancy, we put about *one-sixth* into our arts funding compared to what the European average for cultural funding is, and I want to double-stress the word *average* here. Increasing our funding sixfold would only raise us to par, which is a pathetic and shameful situation to be in.

When compared to the national budget for healthcare in Ireland, the money given to the arts in Ireland was once described by an Irish health-service official as the type of change that they might accidentally find behind the radiator.

You may have no interest in attending a challenging piece of contemporary dance, and you may fucking hate the opera, or you may think that circus isn't a real art in the first place.

That's all fair enough. In fact, if you were to go back seven or eight years, I would probably have agreed with you.

But I know more now – not least because my livelihood is based on it, says you – and what quickly becomes indisputable for anyone who cares to look is that we undervalue artists of all kinds in this country, to a level that almost makes you think that we don't care.

And, in most cases, that's the truth, which is sad.

I'm not the biggest Churchillian who has ever lived, but he pretty much nailed it when he said to the Royal Academy on 30 April 1938: 'The arts are essential to any complete national life. The State owes it to itself to sustain and encourage them … Ill fares the race which fails to salute the arts with the reverence and delight which are their due.'

If Winston Churchill, the quintessential conservative, monarchic, military arch-imperialist can still possess such a fine appreciation for the importance of the arts, then there's no reason why we can't as well.

But I digress.

My misgivings at that time about the wastage of public monies notwithstanding, we applied for funding to tour our show and, once again, we were successful.

This gave us not only the opportunity to take the show all over the country to places like the Dublin Fringe Festival, Cork, Westport, Northern Ireland and a few others, but also the capacity to do more development on it. One of the jewels of our funding proposal had been the Roscommon Arts Centre agreeing to give us three weeks of access to their space to re-stage and redevelop the show ahead of a second premiere in that same venue for this new iteration of *How to Square a Circle*.

We wanted to draw out the narrative conflict within the piece more, to hone the characters' desires and intentions so the story would become clearer and leaner and more satisfying for an audience, to make it more human.

This focus on narrative might be the biggest thing that sets contemporary circus apart from traditional. Traditional circus shows are all about the tricks, how you build up anticipation for them and how well you execute them. In contemporary circus, however, even when it's entirely non-verbal, there's always some semblance of character and a latent idea of story inherent within it. Sometimes this is developed to such an extent that it becomes as much theatre as it is circus, with maybe a healthy portion of dance included. Sometimes it's the opposite, with only a very vague and loose idea of character and narrative, but it's always there in some form.

We wanted to tell a story and tell it well. We'd been happy with what we'd managed the first time around, but with the resources now to bring a director in as a full-time collaborator, we knew we had the opportunity to improve.

The director we chose was an artist called Raymond Keane, a man from a theatre background who already had a thorough familiarity with circus, having done work with Tumble Circus before us, and with his own company, Barrabas, before that.

Similarly, we now had the funds to bring a producer on board who was external to myself or Aisling, and who could shoulder the burden of organising a tour, which is a task that requires a person with the care of a nurse, the business acumen of a tycoon and the patience of a saint as they answer a hundred different questions in a thousand different ways for the different staff of the different venues around the country. This person was Dee Molloy, the same woman who, three years previously, had listened to me spill my guts about my lack of experience to Philly McMahon prior to the *Riot* rehearsals in that quay-side café in Dublin.

These were two people we could trust to look after us and our show. But even at that, we were reticent to hand over the reins to this piece we had created, this show into which we had poured so much of ourselves. What if we gave it to the wrong person and they didn't get it? *How to Square a Circle* wasn't only a show for us; it was a creation, born from ourselves. The notion that another person might come in and harm it was a horrific idea, and we were fearful of it.

Both Dee and Ray were fantastic, thankfully. They helped guide the work into a better place. Creatively, Ray came in with a caring eye that was able to appreciate what we had done, but look at it from a constructively critical position, and slowly iron out the kinks that we weren't able to see since we were too close to it.

In its original form, the show had contained a lot of dialogue, but it was loose and imprecise, and what Ray understood better than us was that circus is much closer to film than it is to theatre, insofar as it works best when you show instead of telling. Show the audience what you feel and show them how you react; they'll understand, and they'll pick up the story. You only need to talk if absolutely necessary.

We quickly found that we barely needed to speak at all; the story was already there, within ourselves and within the show.

The three weeks of redevelopment went well, but there were other fears lurking around this return to Roscommon.

First off, I was coming into the show in Roscommon carrying an injury. It was not the first injury in my circus career, and it certainly was not the first time I'd had to perform while sore because, as I've alluded to previously, circus is a full-tilt profession similar in so many ways to athletic activity. You spend yourself by performing, the risk of injury is high and ever-present, and you cannot train, rehearse or perform without counting the cost in burns, bruises and aching muscles.

But this injury was different. It was the first time I'd had to take some serious time off from performing. I'd tweaked something in between my ribs, which had been innocuous at first, but had worsened. I'd visited a few different medical people over it and had not been able to get a firm answer from any of them. The general consensus had been to give it time and see what happened, which wasn't exactly useful.

As a result, I'd come into our Roscommon rehearsals not entirely certain this tour was something I'd be able to pull off. *How to Square a Circle* is a show that, even under full fitness, pushes me and Aisling right to the edge of our physical and technical limits. There's so much uncertainty throughout as to whether or not we're going to pull something off, which is a danger that gives circus an added thrill for the audience as they understand that failure is distinctly possible, and seeing failure evaded by the performers is part of the enjoyment.

But this general uncertainty was super-charged by my injury, and that nagging doubt had been a nasty resident in the corner of my head all summer: that I might get right to the lip of this thing and then have to pull out. Would this be like my All-Ireland quarter finals all over again? I tried not to think about it. We did our work and hoped for the best.

To compound matters, tickets for the show were selling slowly – very, very slowly. It was so bad that a week before this second premiere, we had a grand total of sixteen tickets sold. This sent me into a panic of furious marketing activity whereby I deluged Facebook with promotions, spending my time poring over the advert analytics in the hope that I might find the key to a Roscommon audience.

I was definitely spooked. All the same, this was a home-coming for me, and I didn't want to lose heart.

There's plenty of artists producing great work who struggle badly to sell tickets to their shows when they visit the less-urbanised areas of the country. They protect themselves, understandably so, by proclaiming that the audiences just aren't there, that there aren't enough people who 'get it', that they were doomed to failure from the very start. Which is fine, I understand it, but it doesn't escape the fact that it sounds like they're saying that country people are stupid, that they're simple and thick. Which is something I entirely disagree with.

Being a hometown boy, and being a product of my environment, I wanted very badly to prove this, to bring the people of my youth and the people of my county together to show them – and anyone else who might be paying attention – what was possible in the art form of circus and in places like Roscommon.

Also, much deeper but equally undeniable, I wanted to succeed in drawing an audience to assure myself that what I'd done in choosing an arts life, and what I was doing in continuing to pursue it, had a worth.

It's entirely correct to have what Blindboy Boatclub from *The Rubberbandits* would term as an 'internal locus of evaluation', an ability to regard the worth of your work from within yourself instead of looking for the validation of external factors. I agree with that wholeheartedly.

But this was my home; my family and my friends. I wanted them to see the show and I wanted them to *get it*. I wanted them to get it because I wanted to be able to connect to them on these new, artistic terms in much the same way I had been able to connect with them in my older life, as a teacher and as a footballer.

Art is about performance. Whether that's a painting on a wall, a story in a book or a show on a stage, it doesn't matter. It only becomes art once someone other than you experiences it. Up until then, it's creative, sure it is, but it's not art.

I wanted to bring my art home. I wanted it to be enjoyed. Was there anything wrong with that? I don't think so.

So, Aisling and I, working closely with the staff of the

Roscommon Arts Centre, put a lot of effort into trying to sell the show. We got spots in local newspapers and radio while we continued to flood social media with notices about the event.

The day before the show, the number had crept up to seventy people, which was okay, but still a good way short of half-capacity for a venue that could fit about one hundred and ninety people.

I have a large extended family, which provided me with an emergency option should the numbers not pick up. But I specifically didn't want to flood the arts centre with the Bradys and the Dowds. I could have done that and I could have packed the house, but that would have masked the point, which was that I wanted to prove that a show like ours, something that was unfamiliar, a show without much dialogue but full of circus and movement, could succeed in a place like Roscommon.

So, I resisted declaring an emergency through the Brady/ Dowd family network, which was just as well because, by the time the night rolled around, we had a full house on our hands and the place was hopping, queues outside the door, which Averyl, the director of the venue, said she'd never seen before.

What happened next was the most amazing experience I've had in my professional life to date.

I'd done big performances before, like *Riot* in Vicar Street, which was a wild and exuberant free-for-all, with the audience drinking and letting themselves loose while we rocked it from the stage. Differently, but of a similar impact, I did a wheel performance during the half-time break between

Roscommon and Leitrim in Hyde Park, which also had a homecoming aspect to it for me. It placed me back in my old footballing context but with my artistic hat squarely on my head, thousands of people watching me perform from the terraces and the feeling that they were all really responding to it.

I'd performed in the Baku Olympic Stadium with seventy thousand people cheering as I flew through the air, suspended in a crescent moon. They were big crowds, great shows and special moments, but none of them compared to what we put on the stage that night in Roscommon.

We began the show sitting in the back row of the audience. We did this from a logistical necessity connected to how we started the show, but it had the unintended bonus of allowing us to get a feel for the energy sizzling across the auditorium that evening. It was palpable, like white-hot sparks cascading from a metalworker's blow torch. There was a thrum from the crowd that we could feel in our stomachs, and once the lights went down we were carried along by a force that was not of our making, but which was channelled by the performance we delivered.

An hour later, as the stage lights faded to dark to signal the end of the show, we hadn't even had a chance to re-emerge for our bow before the audience leapt to their feet and lifted the roof off the place, a thundering roar of hands and voices calling out in delight. Aisling and I stumbled into the middle of the stage to take our bow and stare into the faces of the crowd.

I was just so delighted these people had come and elated that they'd connected with this thing we had made.

There were a few faces I recognised amongst the roar, but most of them were strangers, people completely unknown to me, and yet they had come here anyway, seen the show and been swept up by the same emotion that was now lifting me and Aisling into the fuzzy air of that cool September night.

Averyl came over to us after the show telling us there were so many faces in the audience that were new even to her, people who had never crossed the threshold of the centre before, who had arrived having had to ask directions towards it – *so it's across from the mart, over by the fire station? I know the spot, but I'd never known that there was an arts centre there before*. It was a special night, buoyed by that rare conflux of energies that evolves something from being good into being great.

There's so much to be gotten from art, yet it's so easy to ignore. It's so easy to fall back on our tendency to gravitate towards other, more familiar things. And here we were, amongst the culchies and the thicks as they'd been frequently derided; a packed house of my people in a beautiful building on the edge of Roscommon town.

Don't misunderstand me. I didn't bring them to Jesus. I wasn't some artistic saviour bringing culture to the unwashed. The revelation that happened there was mine, really, not theirs.

I'd come home, a different man from the boy who grew up in the fields of Corrigeen, with so much unearthed from within me since I had left, so much that had needed to be challenged and examined and redirected and healed. It's a process that has barely begun, but one that doesn't really have an end, because as people, we are and will always be works in progress.

***

It's two weeks on from that show now, on this drive back home to Michelle in Athlone, and still I can feel a warm tingle at the thought of what happened that night. I'm looking down at the road in front of me and I'm thinking about the rest of the tour ahead of us. We've already sold out shows in Westport and our entire run for the Dublin Fringe Festival, we have got our largest single audience in The Everyman Theatre in Cork, then we will take the show to Portugal, and we have also been invited to perform it next year in the English National Ballet to an audience of international promoters.

My body is still sore and I still have those doubts. I don't know where my life goes from here. I can't answer a lot of the questions that still swirl within me. The doubts I have remain a constant presence. It's a presence I am trying to learn to be comfortable with, because I think that doubt is an inescapable part of life. Why resist it if it's always going to be there?

One thing I definitely know is that there is always hope for change. I hope I continue to change. I hope I can learn from my own mistakes and those of my father and my family. I hope I can love those closest to me in the way they deserve. I hope I have the strength to face the tough times ahead and the grace to know the good times while they're there. I hope I can stay on this course I have set for myself, and I hope I can see where it leads.

ACKNOWLEDGEMENTS

First and foremost, I would like to thank Patrick O'Donoghue and all the team at Mercier Press for approaching me to write this book and then guiding me through the process. Thank you for entertaining my numerous changes of direction. The book has turned out very different from what we first envisioned, but I'm so glad it did.

Thank you to Gorgeous George, my ghostwriter, who captured my voice and understood my ways more than anyone else could. I cannot thank you enough.

To Jane Russel at Outlaw Management for looking after me throughout the process.

To my family, I love you all dearly. I have written this with as much care as I could while remaining as honest as I can. We are all hurting in some way and at various stages and I hope this helps.

To Michelle: I cannot thank or express my love enough to you. We have grown, changed and evolved together so much over the past fourteen years. I look forward so much to seeing that continue and to sitting beside you in some old folks' home, holding your hand and telling you the same terrible jokes I've been telling you for years.

FOLLOW THE AUTHOR

WEBSITE: WWW.RONANBRADY.ME

PATREON: PATREON.COM/RONANBRADY

 @ANOMALYRONAN

@ANOMALYRONAN

@ANOMALYPERFORMANCE

RONAN BRADY ANOMALY PERFORMANCE